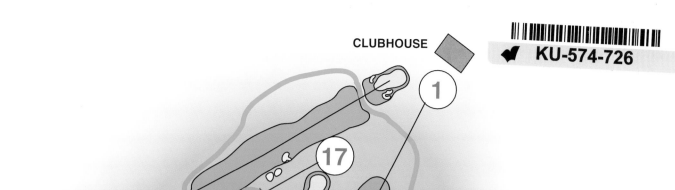

CLUBHOUSE

KU-574-726

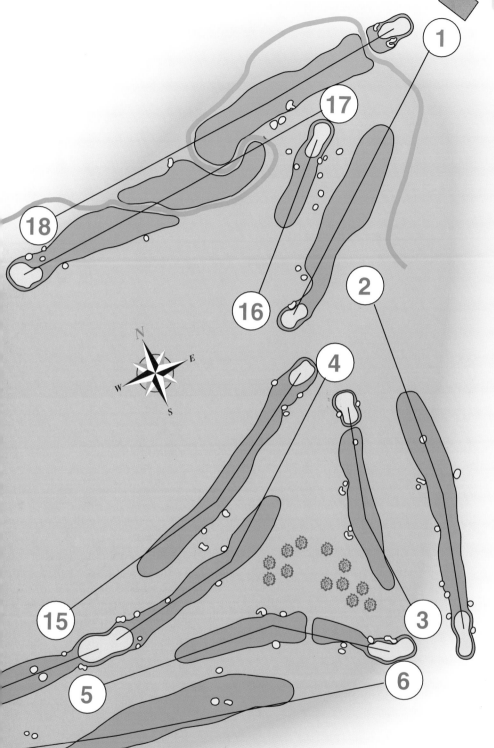

THE OPEN CHAMPIONSHIP
1999

OFFICIAL ANNUAL IN ASSOCIATION WITH

THE OPEN CHAMPIONSHIP 1999

OFFICIAL ANNUAL IN ASSOCIATION WITH

WRITERS

ANDY FARRELL
MICHAEL MCDONNELL
RICHARD SIMMONS
RON SIRAK
ALISTER NICOL
JOHN HOPKINS

PHOTOGRAPHERS

MICHAEL COHEN
FRED VUICH

EDITOR

BEV NORWOOD

AUTHORISED BY THE
CHAMPIONSHIP COMMITTEE
OF THE ROYAL AND ANCIENT
GOLF CLUB OF ST ANDREWS

HAZLETON PUBLISHING LTD
3 Richmond Hill, Richmond, Surrey TW10 6RE

Published 1999 by Hazleton Publishing Ltd
Copyright © 1999 The Championship Committee Merchandising
Limited

Statistics of 128th Open Championship produced on a
Unisys Computer System

Course illustration courtesy of DuCam Marketing (UK) Ltd.

Fred Vuich is staff photographer for GOLF Magazine (USA)
and photographs are courtesy of Times Mirror Magazines, Inc.

Photographs on pages 12, 13, 53 courtesy of Stephen Szurlej,
© The New York Times Company Magazine Group, Inc. All rights reserved.
Photographs on pages 2, 10, 32-34, 64, 88, 91 courtesy of Allsport Photographic Plc.

A CIP catalogue record for this book is available
from the British Library

ISBN: 1-874557-241

Typeset by Davis Design
Printed in Great Britain
by Butler & Tanner, Frome, Somerset

CONTENTS

INTRODUCTION by Sir Richard Evans CBE   7

THE CHAMPIONSHIP COMMITTEE   8

INTRODUCTION by H. M. Campbell   9

FOREWORD by Paul Lawrie   11

ROUND CARNOUSTIE   14

THE VENUE: A DAUNTING PROSPECT by Michael McDonnell   15

FIRST ROUND: A BATTLE IN THE BREEZE by Andy Farrell   21

COMMENTARY: BACK TO THE FUTURE by Richard Simmons   33

SECOND ROUND: PAR FALLS TO DIVERSE FIELD by Andy Farrell   37

COMMENTARY: NO MATCH FOR THE COURSE by Ron Sirak   51

THIRD ROUND: IT'S FIVE SHOTS, BY JEAN by Andy Farrell   55

COMMENTARY: HIGH DRAMA ON THE LINKS by Alister Nicol   69

FOURTH ROUND: GREAT SCOT, WHAT A FINISH by Andy Farrell   73

COMMENTARY: IT JUST HAS TO BE TRUE by John Hopkins   89

OPEN CHAMPIONSHIP RESULTS   93

OPEN CHAMPIONSHIP RECORDS   97

COMPLETE SCORES OF 128th OPEN CHAMPIONSHIP   101

INTRODUCTION

BY SIR RICHARD EVANS CBE

Chief Executive
British Aerospace plc

The return of the Open Championship to Carnoustie after a gap of over 20 years lived up to all our expectations. The course presented a fearsome challenge to the world's greatest golfers and provided spectators with a feast of enjoyment. The thrills and upsets of the closing holes on the final day were straight out of a storybook and the sight of the local hero, Paul Lawrie, clinching his victory with the boldest of shots to the 18th at the end of the play-off was something we will not forget for a long time.

Watching such drama unfold makes me reflect on the uniqueness of the game of golf. In no other sport would you see players cope with the pressure and crushing disappointment that a single bad shot can bring with such control and good humour. The way Jean Van de Velde handled a devastating situation was a huge credit to him personally and the sport he represents.

The unique spirit which golf encourages is one reason why British Aerospace is proud to continue its sponsorship of National Golf Week in association with the Professional Golfers' Association. In 1999, National Golf Week attracted a record level of interest with over 25,000 people taking the opportunity of having lessons with their local golf professionals. Hopefully, many of these will now take up the sport and experience for themselves the enjoyment it offers.

Finally, may I congratulate the Royal and Ancient Golf Club and the Championship Committee at Carnoustie for a tremendous event. I hope that we can look forward to another exciting tournament back at Carnoustie before too long.

Sir Richard Evans CBE

THE CHAMPIONSHIP COMMITTEE

CHAIRMAN

H. M. CAMPBELL

DEPUTY CHAIRMAN

R. M. BURNS

COMMITTEE

P. E. BECHMANN
J. J. N. CAPLAN
M. C. GRINT
J. M. KIPPAX
A. J. N. LOUDON
M. S. R. LUNT
P. D. MONTGOMERY
R. D. MUCKART
J. L. S. PASQUILL
N. M. STEPHENS
M. C. TATE

ADDITIONAL MEMBER

M. N. DOYLE
COUNCIL OF NATIONAL GOLF UNIONS

SECRETARY

SIR MICHAEL BONALLACK, OBE

CHAMPIONSHIP SECRETARY

D. HILL

ASSISTANT SECRETARY (CHAMPIONSHIPS)

D. R. WEIR

ASSISTANT SECRETARY (CHAMPIONSHIPS)

A. E. FARQUHAR

INTRODUCTION

BY H. M. CAMPBELL
Chairman of Championship Committee
Royal and Ancient Golf Club of St Andrews

Carnoustie's reputation as one of the toughest golf courses in the world was confirmed in the 128th Open Championship. The mild and wet weather in the weeks leading up to the Championship resulted in a deep and heavy rough bordering an already long and narrow layout with the result that the course would find out anyone who did not come there at the top of their game. With strong winds blowing on the first two days, Carnoustie presented as tough a test as any Open in recent history.

Congratulations go to the three players who contested the play-off, champion Paul Lawrie, Jean Van de Velde and Justin Leonard, who outlasted the strong challenges of others such as Greg Norman, Tiger Woods and Davis Love III.

Paul Lawrie won the hard way, having started in the Final Qualifying and then coming from a record 10 strokes behind the leader in the last round. His marvelous 67 equaled the lowest score of the Championship, and he won with birdies on the final two holes of the play-off. He became the first Scot to win in Scotland for 68 years, since Tommy Armour.

The Royal and Ancient Championship Committee are very grateful for the support from the many sources necessary for a successful Championship, starting with the Regional and Final Qualifying Clubs, together with the Carnoustie Golf Links Championship Committee and Angus Council, all of whom contributed significantly.

The continued support of British Aerospace for this official Annual is also appreciated, along with the work of the photographers and writers whose contributions appear on the following pages.

H. M. Campbell

FOREWORD

BY PAUL LAWRIE

Winning any Open Championship would be special, but winning at Carnoustie was a dream come true for me. I wasn't wishing ill on Jean Van de Velde, but he obviously made a couple of mistakes coming in and I played lovely in the play-off. To birdie the last two holes to win was like a fairy story.

I went to a few Opens when I was younger, and I think every kid dreams about winning the Open. It's a huge thing for anyone to do, especially when you win in Scotland and you live nearby. Everyone was shouting me on. The play-off was just incredible.

The golf course was very, very tough, but it's a major championship and you should pass the exam. I had a feeling that someone inexperienced could win because the fairways were narrow, the rough knee-deep, and a lot of the leading players had complained. Being accustomed to strong winds and links courses, I went there believing I could play well and compete.

Then, 10 shots back, I didn't think I had any hope, but strange things happen, especially round here, when the course is so tough. I didn't have any problem with the golf course set-up. I just went ahead and did my job, and when my chance came I was prepared.

Paul Lawrie

The Barry Burn is in play twice on the 18th hole, running down the right side, sweeping across the fairway then back.

ROUND CARNOUSTIE

No 1 407 Yards, Par 4

The first is not as gentle as it first appears, because fairway contours push even the best-placed tee shot towards the sand hills and bunkers on the right. It is invariably played against the westerly wind.

No 2 462 Yards, Par 4

Braid's Bunker lurks 220 yards from the tee and the approach must be threaded through a narrow corridor of fairway to an equally narrow—and long—green protected by humps, hollows, bunkers and rough.

No 3 342 Yards, Par 4

The shortest par-4 but one of the deadliest because of the threat from fairway bunkers and Jockie's Burn, which runs close to the green. The sensible route follows the left side of the fairway to take rough and dunes out of play.

No 4 412 Yards, Par 4

It is a formidable driving hole into the prevailing westerly wind, with bunkers strategically placed where the fairway turns to the right. There is not much safety on the left either, because Jockie's Burn flanks most of it.

No 5 411 Yards, Par 4

Fairway bunkers in the left rough—new to the 1999 Open Championship—force tee shots to the right, and Jockie's Burn crosses the fairway 280 yards from the tee. The green is double-tiered.

No 6 578 Yards, Par 5

The brave line is to the left of the three bunkers to find the narrow strip of fairway that is close to the left-hand out-of-bounds fence, so that the second shot is played away from trouble towards the green.

No 7 412 Yards, Par 4

There is more out of bounds on the left, and if the wind blows, a normally generous fairway becomes extremely difficult to hold, making the second shot to a shallow green much more of a problem.

No 8 183 Yards, Par 3

A narrow green that is heavily protected by bunkers can also become an elusive target in a crosswind, particularly with out of bounds to the left and the ever-present long grass all around.

No 9 474 Yards, Par 4

The Nicklaus Bunker is just within driving range and replaces a mound that once stood there until Jack questioned its fairness. Even without this hazard, the out of bounds left and rough to the right represent a fearsome prospect.

No 10 466 Yards, Par 4

Four fairway bunkers menace the landing area and the Barry Burn stretches across the fairway in front of the green and thence along the right-hand side to afford very little margin for error.

No 11 383 Yards, Par 4

An accurate tee shot to a narrow fairway is essential to offer a reasonable chance of finding the contoured green set among bunkers, gorse and hillocks.

No 12 479 Yards, Par 4

Bunkers and a ditch on the right force the tee shot left and the approach must be guided through a gap between bunkered ridges to a wide green that slopes away from the front.

No 13 169 Yards, Par 3

Club choice is vital, because the green climbs a gentle slope some 40 yards from front to back then falls away. Bunkers left and right mean there is no option but to find the putting surface from the tee.

No 14 515 Yards, Par 5

The infamous Spectacles are so named because of the twin bunkers on the left, 70 yards from the green. The correct line from the tee must be to the right, but more sand traps await the errant approach to the green.

No 15 472 Yards, Par 4

The judicious line from the tee is to the left so the ball is gathered back to the middle of the fairway. Otherwise, an approach from the right is blind over rough to a sunken green.

No 16 250 Yards, Par 3

The raised green is long, narrow and well-bunkered, especially at the front, thereby making it a fearsome target with such massive penalties for error including the Barry Burn nearby.

No 17 459 Yards, Par 4

The Barry Burn loops twice across the fairway, creating an island which can be reached only with a powerful drive against the wind. The green slopes towards bunkers on the right.

No 18 487 Yards, Par 4

The Barry Burn comes into play twice. There is rough down both sides of the fairway, with out of bounds flanking the left. More crucially, the burn swings back across the fairway to offer a final threat 30 yards from the green.

A DAUNTING PROSPECT

BY MICHAEL McDONNELL

There is historical neatness about the return of the Open Championship at the end of the 20th century to the modest Scottish town that can really take credit for giving the game to the world at the beginning of it.

More than 300 young men left Carnoustie by the early 1900s to teach and play golf around the world. Most of them landed in the United States, although one hapless émigré bound for South America had such a boisterous farewell party that he slept it off in a bunker and, when he awoke, decided not to make the trip after all.

The distinguished golf essayist Herbert Warren Wind defined the significance of Carnoustie in the global development of the game when he observed: "St Andrews may be the home of golf but Carnoustie is the home of Australian and American professional golf."

Such missionary zeal brought its own rewards, particularly for the Smith brothers who were among the first transatlantic voyagers and dominated American golf in the early years, with Willie winning the US Open in 1899 and brother Alex taking the title in 1906 and 1910, when he beat another brother, Macdonald, in a play-off.

Another son of Carnoustie was to have even greater, if indirect, impact on the history of the game when he took a job at the East Lake Club in Atlanta and taught a young man named Bobby Jones to play. There was even a suggestion that Stewart Maiden had given Jones an identifiable "Carnoustie swing"— a measured, loose and slightly wristy technique that had been born from years of combat against the sturdy elements that regularly assail the links which stand on the north shore of the Tay almost opposite St Andrews to the south.

Maiden remained Jones' only mentor throughout his career and by an ironic twist of fate even the great Grand Slam year of 1930 had a tenuous Carnoustie link because Macdonald Smith finished runner-up to Jones in both the Open and the US Open. Indeed that particular Smith brother went to his grave still regarded as the best golfer of his time never to win a major title, although he did capture the prestigious Los Angeles Open four times in seven years from 1928.

Carnoustie is therefore part of the fabric of the game with a history that extends back into the 1500s when "the gowff" was played at the Barry Links nearby. By 1839 Allan Robertson, generally regarded as the first golf professional, laid out 10 holes and by 1867 Old Tom Morris had extended it to the full 18.

That year, too, his son Young Tom Morris made his winning debut as a professional at the age of 16 at Carnoustie when, according to reports, he "played against and defeated all comers" and thereby added his name to an illustrious list of legends who had graced the formidable links with their exploits.

Carnoustie is at once both magnificent and brutal, majestic and unforgiving. It seems reluctant to yield a score and fights the golfer, particularly over the closing stretch by means of the menacing Barry Burn snaking across fairways to protect its reputation. Even in becalmed conditions it is a daunting prospect and one that offers no respite.

Sir Michael Bonallack, leading amateur in the 1968 Open there, observed, "When the wind is blowing it is probably the toughest golf course in Britain. And even when it's not blowing, it's still the toughest."

When Walter Hagen first played Carnoustie he judged it to be the best course in Britain and one of the best three in the world, which is all the more surprising because it is a flat, long and extremely exposed stretch of unremitting terrain. Yet therein lies its challenge, because Carnoustie requires imagination, invention and determination.

The second, the first of many long par-4s, is protected by humps, hollows, bunkers and rough.

When such qualities are exhibited to the full, then Carnoustie can be engaged in fairly even combat, because of all the Open Championship venues it is the one demanding most respect. When Ben Hogan was asked in later years to reflect on his 1953 victory there, he remarked that he learned very quickly it was unwise to play aggressively because the course could not be overpowered, but had to be tackled diligently while waiting for scoring chances to present themselves.

Hogan's win was remarkable for many reasons, not least of which was the exhaustive preparation he put into his one and only title attempt, despite still suffering the after-effects of his near-fatal car crash, but also because the achievement created a modern professional Grand Slam—how appropriate that it should occur at Carnoustie—in that he won the US Masters, US Open and the Open in the same season but did not compete in the remaining major event—the USPGA Championship.

His 1953 triumph has gathered a subsequent legend all of its own, because of the varied and diverse aspects of his single-minded campaign which began two weeks before the event was scheduled to start. In practice rounds he hit three balls from every tee except the short holes to determine the best position for the approach shot.

Not so however on the notorious sixth, where he struck five tee shots each day to make absolutely sure he could not run into the bunkers that menaced the drive and that he could place the ball precisely between those bunkers and the narrow strip of fairway adjacent to the out-of-bounds fence. It became known as Hogan's Alley because he chose the same route unerringly every round.

His other habit, according to legend, was to walk the course in reverse—from green to tee—each evening to give himself a different perspective on the hazards and their positions, as well as their comparative threats in differing wind conditions. Then he would climb into his chauffeur-driven limousine for the journey back to a private house in Dundee, having previously checked out of the Bruce Hotel because there were no en suite facilities for him to take much-needed hot baths to ease the pains in his legs after play.

He was, of course, a remote figure who remained at arm's length from the Press. There is a story told of one enterprising golf writer who decided to secure an exclusive interview and waited until Hogan had finished his practice session one evening, then explained to the great man that he was stranded and asked for a lift back to Dundee. Hogan said, "That will not be possible." One stranded golf writer. No story. And no lift home either.

These days the excitement that he brought to the

Three bunkers guard the approach from the right of the sixth green, and the narrow, brave line is to the left.

Bunkers on the ninth, out of bounds left and rough to the right represent a fearsome prospect.

The Barry Burn loops twice on the 17th, and the green slopes towards the bunkers on the right.

championship can only be imagined, but a sense of the anticipation was captured eloquently by the late Pat Ward-Thomas, in his book *Master of Golf,* when he wrote: "The wind stood strong from the west; the flags strained at their masts and a great multitude was gathered about the first hole at Carnoustie.

"There was a tension and expectancy abroad and a sense of history such as I have never known at the outset of a championship. On the tee, awaiting his call from the starter, stood the slight grey figure of Hogan, the man who had become a legend in the minds of golfers all over the world."

Hogan was not the first of the game's great figures to answer effectively the challenge that Carnoustie laid down. Tommy Armour had met it in 1931, and in 1937 Henry Cotton scored what he considered to be the best of his three championship wins when he faced a field of supreme quality, as almost the entire US Ryder Cup squad stayed on to compete after their win at Southport.

Thus Cotton found himself facing Byron Nelson, Horton Smith, Sam Snead, Ralph Guldahl, Densmore Shute, Walter Hagen and Johnny Revolta amongst others whose presence added stature to his victory. More than this, Cotton also had to cope with monsoon-like conditions which swept the course and flooded the greens so badly there was doubt whether the contest could be finished on the day.

Indeed, the first pairing in the final round which included Percy Alliss, father of the esteemed television commentator Peter, refused to play on until the first green was cleared of excess water. Bernard Darwin wrote in *Country Life* magazine: "... all through the afternoon the authorities were on tenterhooks and if anybody had lodged a formal appeal against these conditions I think it must have been upheld."

All of which endorsed the brilliance of Cotton's display, because he produced scores of 72 and 71 on the final day for a 290 total to win by two strokes, even taking 5 at the last hole by deliberately leaving his greenside bunker shot short of the hole for fear of thinning his recovery out of bounds on the left.

When Gary Player arrived a week before the championship in 1968, he told waiting Press men that he had never played so well for so long without winning a tournament. However, he held the conviction that sooner or later his luck would change, and Carnoustie was to prove him right.

In the final round he was engaged in a fierce tussle with playing companion Jack Nicklaus, while Billy Casper and Bob Charles had drawn level with him as he played the 14th and tugged his tee shot left behind

The out-of-bounds fence is close on the 18th fairway, and the Barry Burn comes back before the green.

the Spectacles bunkers.

It was his next magnificent stroke that put the title beyond reach of his rivals, as he lashed the ball to the green he could not see, then heard the gathering cheers reach a crescendo of delight. When he reached the green, he saw the reason. This ball was only two feet from the hole and he tapped in for an eagle 3 then picked a cautious route to victory and his second Open title.

Carnoustie was also to play a pivotal role in the distinguished career of Tom Watson, because it was the scene of his arrival into the company of champions after a series of worrying near-misses when victory chances in his own country seemed to go begging.

Moreover, he was to match Ben Hogan's record of winning at his first attempt, although unlike Hogan he came back time and time again, winning a tally of five titles, only one fewer than the record set by Harry Vardon. It was the start of a remarkable period in which he became a dominant figure in the game by winning a total of eight major titles in a 10-year stretch including the US Masters twice and the US Open once.

His Carnoustie success held a sad counterpoint of what-might-have-been for Australian Jack Newton, who faced the American golfer in a play-off and was still tied with him as they played the last hole until Newton bunkered his approach and failed to get down in two. A few years later Newton was to eyewitness the birth of another international star when he finished runner-up to Seve Ballesteros in the US Masters.

The history of Carnoustie is therefore one of unbroken professional achievement, which makes it more than just a monument for glories past, but gives it a clear relevance to each generation of golfers from the time Scots-born Tommy Armour—then an American citizen—held the trophy aloft after victory in the 1931 championship.

In a sense Armour, an Edinburgh University graduate and World War I army hero who was blinded in the left eye, was first to display the qualities that Carnoustie demands and all successive champions have possessed. Bernard Darwin recognised them when he wrote in *Country Life* at the time of Armour's win: "He is full of imagination, a bundle of quivering nerves kept fiercely under control and this is the kind of temperament that either breaks a player of games or makes him terribly formidable." The champions of Carnoustie continue to underline that truth. So do some of the losers, too.

With birdies of 40 and 30 feet on the second and fifth holes, Bernhard Langer posted 72 to share second place.

A BATTLE IN THE BREEZE

BY ANDY FARRELL

When talking to someone from Carnoustie, you quickly notice there is one word missing from their vocabulary. The word "wind" never passes their lips. "Aye, it's just a wee breeze," they will say when the Angus coast is being buffeted by anything up to a full-scale gale. Colin Montgomerie, a Scotsman from the west rather than the east coast, caught the theme on the first day of the 128th Open Championship when he said it was "just a breezy summer's day."

Well, he was almost right. There was not the sort of howling gale that can sweep across the Barry headland that is home to the three Carnoustie courses. But, in any golfer's language, there was a stiff wind blowing to welcome the world's best players back to Carnoustie for the first time in 24 years. It completed a third triad of devils the competitors faced on what is known as the Medal Course, whose fairways have always been narrow but have not always been lined by quite such thick rough, a result of more than a month's rain and sunshine.

"I feel like I've fought a war," commented American Hal Sutton.

"That's the nearest I've come to playing rugby on a links," said Greg Turner of New Zealand.

"I need a stiff drink," added England's Lee Westwood.

When Rodney Pampling, a 29-year-old Australian, completed his round shortly before noon, he became the first player to match Carnoustie's strict par of 71. Almost 10 hours later, he had become the only player to match par.

"I knew it was a good score, but I didn't realise I would be leading at the end of the day," Pampling said that evening. "It was nice to sit back at home and watch everyone else struggle on television."

Pampling began his round at 7.25, along with Bernhard Langer and Steve Pate. Langer scored 72 to share second place with Scott Dunlap, while Pate had 73, two over par, to be joint fourth along with Sutton, Mark McNulty, Dudley Hart, Len Mattiace, Justin Leonard, the 1997 champion at Royal Troon, and the Aberdeen-born Paul Lawrie.

On a day when the average score was 78.31, or seven over par, others could be well satisfied with their day's efforts as well. Montgomerie was one of those on three over after 74, as were Tiger Woods, Davis Love III and Ernie Els. Two-time champion Greg Norman and Tom Lehman, the 1996 winner, had 76s, as did Westwood, Darren Clarke and Ian Woosnam.

Masters champion Jose Maria Olazabal and Nick Faldo had 78s, while on 79 were Payne Stewart, the US Open champion, and the runner-up at Pinehurst, Phil Mickelson, plus David Duval. The world's No 2-ranked golfer, Duval had the consolation that of those who scored eight over or worse, he was one of only three players, Carlos Franco and Tim Herron were the others, to avoid having a double bogey or worse on his card.

Out of the starting field of 156, some 57 failed to break 80. Tom Watson, the 1975 champion at Carnoustie, scored 82, the same as Zane Scotland, an Englishman despite his name who just a few days before his 17th birthday was one of the youngest players ever to come through Regional and Final Qualifying. "This was the easy wind," Watson said of the westerly. "If it was blowing in the opposite direction, well … it would be tougher."

Mark O'Meara had handled the wind superbly at Royal Birkdale the year before, but now the defending champion, he slipped to 83. He had three double bogeys and a triple bogey. Not since Bob Ferguson, in 1882 when the Open was decided over 36 holes, had a defending champion had such a poor start and gone on to retain his title. "It does hurt your pride to shoot in the 80s," O'Meara said. "I mean, I'm a

Rodney Pampling was level par in his Open debut.　　　Scott Dunlap (72) benefited from an early start.

professional golfer. But I felt I got the score I deserved today."

Sergio Garcia was not so accepting of his fate. The 19-year-old Spaniard, who won the amateur honours at Augusta in April, had exploded onto the professional scene. Only two weeks before the Open he won his maiden PGA European Tour event, the Murphy's Irish Open, with a stunning final round of 64. A few days later he opened at Loch Lomond with 62 and eventually finished as runner-up to Montgomerie. All eyes were on the former British Amateur champion, but if Norman thought it was "like climbing Mount Everest" after a double-bogey 6 at the first, what could Garcia be thinking after starting with a 7?

"It does cross your mind that you'd like to walk off," he admitted.

Fortunately, wise counsel in the form of his caddie, Jerry Higginbotham, who previously worked for O'Meara, prevailed. Garcia set himself the goal of breaking 80, but with four double bogeys he only just broke 90. His 89 was "beaten" only by Tom Gillis' 90 and the 91 from Prayad Marksaeng, the only Thai golfer to qualify to play in the Open.

Such was the clamour that by the end of the day the Royal and Ancient officials were explaining it was not their intent to tie competitors in knots or embarrass them. Nor had fertiliser been put on the rough to make it grow so tangly. "We don't set out to make the players look like idiots," said Sir Michael Bonallack, Secretary of the R and A. "Carnoustie has lived up to its reputation as the hardest championship course. We don't like seeing players struggle, but this is a test of character as well as golf."

One look at the leaderboard, however, showed the advantage of an early tee time. The wind did not take long to get up, but the time spent on the practice range and over the first few holes to get into a rhythm was well spent by a number of the early starters. McNulty, who birdied the first two holes, was in the first group. Pampling, Langer and Pate were next off. Dunlap was in the sixth group of the day and Hart the seventh. Sutton and Leonard, however, went off just before one o'clock, and Mattiace and Lawrie in successive groups well after three o'clock, making their efforts particularly worthy.

Langer holed from 40 feet and 30 feet for birdies at the second and fifth holes, but then took a double-

The first man out, Australian Peter O'Malley (76) birdied the second hole, but was five over par after nine.

Patrik Sjoland (74) was three under after four holes.

Andrew Coltart (74) was two under after 14 holes.

Davis Love III (74) went out in 35, but took 6 at the 12th.

bogey 7 at the par-5 sixth. This was a sign of things to come and at 578 yards, into the wind, the hole Ben Hogan mastered during his victory in 1953 was to play as one of the hardest on the course. Langer drove into the right rough, played up the right rough, switched over to the left rough, then back to the right rough before finding the green and two-putting.

"You can argue about some of the other holes, but the sixth is the one I think is unfair," said the German. "The lay-up area is only 11 yards wide."

Langer is one of the best managers of his game in difficult conditions and described the challenge presented by Carnoustie's 7,361 yards thus: "It is the longest course I think we've ever played and yet there are so many holes you can't hit driver on because it is just too narrow. It's not percentage golf at all."

Langer's outward nine of 35, one under, was only matched by Love. Pampling went out in 36, mainly thanks to a short game that made sure he had only 10 putts despite finding only the sixth green in regulation figures. Eschewing a driver for much of the round, he played the hole with two "driving irons" and a six iron. "My driving iron has a loft of 18 degrees and goes about 180 into the wind and 300 down wind," Pampling said.

The Australian parred the first 11 holes but then only had two more to finish. His first dropped shot came at the 12th, where he drove into the rough, wedged out, but missed the green with his third. The damage was repaired with a nine iron to 10 feet at the short 13th and then, at the 515-yard 14th, playing downwind, Pampling hit his driving iron and a six iron to 25 feet and holed the putt for an eagle to go two under par.

The last four holes destroyed many a card and Pampling's dropped shots at the 15th and 17th were better than most achieved. "I don't mind the wind," Pampling said. "My ball flight is generally low anyway, so I don't have to worry about keeping it low, and it makes you think a lot harder. The course was playing extremely hard. If you don't hit the fairways you are looking at bogey straightaway, if not worse."

This was Pampling's first visit to the Open and followed his maiden victory on the Australasian Tour earlier in the year at the Canon Challenge in Sydney. Having grown up in the Queensland farming town of Caboolture, Pampling did a three-year apprenticeship greenkeeping to get out of school.

He turned professional in 1992 but struggled for a number of years before meeting Angela, a psychologist whom he married in April. "She has done wonders for me," he said. "The drills Angela has taught me have been a big help. She has taught me breathing techniques, counting to calm myself, and walking more slowly, all designed to minimise bad feelings."

The techniques would be needed by Pampling the following day, but others required them on this Thursday. Patrik Sjoland of Sweden was the only player to get to three under par. He did so by birdieing the first, third and fourth holes. "I was playing really solid but I took a wrong line off the fifth tee," Sjoland said. A double bogey there and a triple bogey at the 17th gave Sjoland 74. His five birdies for the round was only equalled by Els.

Andrew Coltart got to two under with a birdie at the 14th, but then dropped five strokes over the last four holes, including a 6 at the 17th. "I was surprised

Hal Sutton (73) had double bogey on the seventh.

to find myself two under par," said Coltart, from Dumfries in the southwest of Scotland. "It helps having grown up playing in conditions like this. You know everyone is going to have a nightmare. You are just trying not to take it too seriously."

Derrick Cooper, the veteran PGA European Tour player from England, was one under with four to play but finished bogey, par, triple bogey, bogey. His only bad drive of the round was at the 17th and it finished in the Barry Burn. His third finished in a bush and his first hack out moved the ball only three feet.

Spain's Miguel Angel Martin bettered Pampling's run of pars with 15 of them, but then bogeyed the last three holes.

The fifth eagle of the day at the Spectacles, the 14th, by Jean Van de Velde brought the Frenchman back to level par, but he bogeyed the next two and took a 6 at 17. His 75 was two shots worse than the 73s of the two men with whom his destiny would be entwined three days later, Leonard and Lawrie.

For Leonard, playing the second nine in level par in difficult conditions on the first day two years ago

Justin Leonard (73) was happy but for a three-putt 14th.

Tiger Woods (74) saved par from the rough at the 12th.

at Royal Troon had been a vital ingredient in his Open triumph. This time, the American managed to get home in one over, parring in from the 13th. "I am very pleased with the way I played, the way I hit the ball and how, mentally, I handled the conditions," Leonard said.

"Patience was a big key. There are so many things you have to factor into each shot, after 72 holes here, I think the guys are going to need a few days off."

The young American had taken the opportunity, over the practice days, to savour some of the history of the town, especially that relating to the late Hogan. Leonard represents the equipment company founded by the 1953 Open champion. "This is a special place and it means a lot that Mr Hogan did so well here," Leonard said. "I was walking back from dinner two days ago and a gentleman stopped me and talked about Mr Hogan for 20 minutes. He was so excited, I worried he was going to have heart palpitations."

With a late tee time, Lawrie was able to have a lie-in at home in Aberdeen, an hour by car up the coast north of Carnoustie, and watch some of the golf on television before setting out for work. By the time the

30-year-old had finished, at 8.40 pm, his card showed only three bogeys and a birdie at the 12th.

As well as the hazards faced by everyone else, Lawrie had the added distractions of a cool evening, plus the noise of various people packing up and the waste collection vans moving in. "That was the draw I was given and you just have to get on with it," he said. "I've no complaints and would take 73 every day round here."

As far as distractions go, Woods had what might have been the most worrying but turned out to be the most enjoyable. As the world's No 1 player lined up his putt at the 18th, a scantily clad woman, dressed only in bra and knickers, ran onto the green to give Tiger a hug and a kiss. Yvonne Robb, a 20-year-old dancer, then spent the night at the pleasure of the Arbroath Constabulary.

The first hint for Woods that something was happening as he was crouching over the line of his putt came from one of his playing partners, Ian Woosnam. "I looked up and Woosie was laughing," Woods explained. "He was still chuckling and then all of a sudden I saw these feet run by. With my spikes, I

Naomichi Ozaki (74) took 6 at the sixth and 7 at the 14th.

Katsuyoshi Tomori (74) had 6 at the 12th, then two birdies.

David Duval (79) posted nines of 39 and 40.

Ernie Els (74) equalled the day's best with five birdies.

Colin Montgomerie (74) battled back after going three over par after eight holes.

didn't want to step on her bare feet. She gave me a hug and a kiss and ran off.

"I guess my first instinct was to protect myself, but luckily she didn't have a whole lot on and her hands were up so she wasn't holding anything, so I assumed it was a pretty benign situation. It could have been more dangerous if someone had more on or had a hand obviously behind their back or something like that."

For the record, Tiger's putt came up just short of the hole. The birdie would have made up in part for bogeys at the 16th and 17th. His only birdie of the round came with a two-putt at the 14th but he had no worse than a bogey on his card. His game plan was to steer his way around the course and only used the driver at the fourth which cost his first bogey.

"I hit some pretty weird clubs off the tees but I kept the ball in play beautifully and just wasn't able to make the birdie putts," Woods said. "You have to stay away from the high numbers."

Woods had won three of his four tournaments prior to the Open. Montgomerie was also bang in form after winning his first event in Scotland, at Loch Lomond, the previous weekend. "Last week's win has relaxed me into trying to enjoy this championship more than in previous years," Monty said. His record of only one top-10 finish in nine Opens was not one to write home about. Despite a double-bogey 5 at the short eighth, he was happy with 74.

"I'll take three more of them," he said. "It seems crazy I know that plus-12 could be a winning score but it doesn't matter how much over par you are this week, as long as you are one less than the rest.

"Today was more about courage than skill and for me to be three over after eight and to hang on to still be three over now was good. Forgetting the score, this is the best position I've been in and the best I've felt going into a second day. Mind you, with my record in the Open that's not saying very much. But a lot of good players have been blown away today and there will be more tomorrow and more on Saturday and more on Sunday."

About that, Montgomerie was spot on, as would be seen over the next three days.

Graeme Storm (82) played as Amateur champion.

Zane Scotland (82) was, at 16, the youngest competitor.

Defending champion Mark O'Meara (83) started poorly.

US Open champion Payne Stewart (79) had one birdie.

FIRST ROUND RESULTS

HOLE	1	2	3	4	5	6	7	8	9	10	11	12	13	14	15	16	17	18	
PAR	4	4	4	4	4	5	4	3	4	4	4	4	3	5	4	3	4	4	TOTAL
Rodney Pampling	4	4	4	4	4	5	4	3	4	4	4	5	2	3	5	3	5	4	71
Bernhard Langer	4	3	4	4	3	7	4	2	4	4	5	4	3	4	4	4	5	4	72
Scott Dunlap	4	4	4	3	4	6	4	3	4	4	4	4	3	4	5	4	4	4	72
Mark McNulty	3	3	4	4	4	6	4	3	5	4	5	5	3	5	3	4	4	4	73
Steve Pate	4	4	5	3	5	5	4	3	4	5	4	4	3	4	3	3	5	5	73
Dudley Hart	5	4	3	5	3	5	6	3	5	4	4	4	3	4	4	4	3	4	73
Hal Sutton	4	4	4	5	3	5	6	2	4	4	4	3	4	5	4	4	4	73
Justin Leonard	4	4	3	4	4	6	5	3	4	4	4	5	3	5	4	3	4	4	73
Len Mattiace	4	4	4	5	5	5	4	3	3	4	4	4	3	4	5	4	3	5	73
Paul Lawrie	4	4	4	4	4	5	5	3	4	4	4	3	4	5	5	3	4	4	73

HOLE SUMMARY

HOLE	PAR	EAGLES	BIRDIES	PARS	BOGEYS	HIGHER	RANK	AVERAGE
1	4	0	9	93	44	10	14	4.37
2	4	0	10	100	38	8	15	4.28
3	4	0	5	109	37	5	16	4.27
4	4	0	8	87	53	8	13	4.40
5	4	0	11	77	57	11	11	4.46
6	5	0	4	76	58	18	3	5.59
7	4	1	9	79	43	24	5	4.52
8	3	0	11	80	57	8	12	3.41
9	4	0	4	62	66	24	1	4.74
OUT	36	1	71	763	453	116		40.02
10	4	1	10	73	56	16	7	4.50
11	4	0	9	77	59	11	10	4.47
12	4	0	7	77	52	20	4	4.55
13	3	0	16	111	27	2	17	3.10
14	5	5	77	54	17	3	18	4.59
15	4	0	8	71	70	7	8	4.49
16	3	0	3	81	66	6	9	3.48
17	4	0	8	70	59	19	2	4.62
18	4	0	10	79	50	17	6	4.51
IN	35	6	148	693	456	101		38.29
TOTAL	71	7	219	1456	909	217		78.31

Players Below Par			0
Players At Par			1
Players Above Par			155

WEATHER
Temperature: low 11°C, high 26°C.
Strong southwest breeze.

LOW SCORES

Low First Nine	Bernhard Langer	35
	Davis Love III	35
Low Second Nine	Dudley Hart	34
	Santiago Luna	34
	Brian Watts	34
Low Round	Rodney Pampling	71

Although he won in 1975, Tom Watson said, "To tell the truth, I didn't much care for the links concept right away."

COMMENTARY

BACK TO THE FUTURE

BY RICHARD SIMMONS

Twenty-four years after they contested the last 18-hole play-off in the history of the Open Championship, Tom Watson and Jack Newton made an emotional return to the rippling links of Carnoustie.

Given that we're talking about Watson, a man to whom the history and the traditions of the game far outweigh anything else in golf, it was surprising to learn that the staging of the 128th Open Championship marked his first return to Carnoustie since 1975. This, after all, is where Tom first discovered the mystery of links golf.

"To tell the truth, I didn't much care for the links concept right away," says Watson, nearly a quarter of a century on. "I can remember arriving at Carnoustie for a practice round on the Monday and being told by Keith Mackenzie that we couldn't play, because the course was reserved for qualifiers. So John Mahaffey and I ended up playing down the road, at Monifieth, which was a rude shock. I didn't much care for pot bunkers, sideways bounces and a wind that just wouldn't quit. I truly didn't like the game over here until Royal Lytham in 1979, when I finally realised you simply had to adapt to survive, and accept the challenge." By then he had won the Open twice.

In full battle dress, Carnoustie was never likely to make many new friends this time around, either. Reinstated as an Open venue after 24 years in the doldrums, the venerable Angus links was even longer and tougher than Watson remembered it to be. And none of the changes that had been made in the time that had elapsed between his maiden victory and his return to the last Open of the 20th century were designed to make scoring any easier. At 7,361 yards,

Jack Newton doesn't dwell on the past and remains positive.

it was the longest in championship history, the rough was rougher, the fairways tighter.

"I shot 69 in the first round here in 1975, so I guess you could say it's 13 shots tougher," surmised Watson, after signing for an 82 on Thursday. "It's an unfair course from the standpoint that the fairways are too narrow," he continued. "But Bobby Jones said golf was not meant to be a fair game. If you don't hit it on the fairways you are going to make a lot of bogeys."

In all, nine bogeys and a double bogey (at the 10th) smarted Watson's opening card, including the obligatory 4 at the 245-yard par-3 16th, a hole at which he had now failed to match par in six attempts. A valiant second-round 73, played in a gusting wind on Friday, that had seen Watson reel off three birdies in the last five holes (one, ironically, at the 16th), was not enough to prevent the 49-year-old American from missing the cut by one shot. "It has been an emotional return," he said shortly after learning his fate. "I knew I had to birdie the 18th to have any chance of making the cut and I couldn't help but compare that with the situation in 1975, when I figured I needed a birdie to get into a play-off."

That Watson had that opportunity at all came along as something of a surprise to Jack Newton, then a 25-year-old Australian playing in the last group out with the South African, Bobby Cole. A multiple winner in Europe, and a regular fixture on the US and African tours in the 1970s, Newton was a powerful, flamboyant golfer, and, after a putting tip from Jack Nicklaus during practice, he had been striding the Angus links with a confidence that

Newton led by two in 1975 with four holes to play.

matched his trousers. A course-record 65 in the third round (witnessed, coincidentally, by Nicklaus) had placed Newton just one shot behind the 54-hole leader, Cole; with four holes to play in the final round on Saturday, the Australian was two ahead.

"Standing on the 15th tee I thought the claret jug was on its way Down Under," he says. "But three straight bogeys did me in. I was busy hacking my way down the 17th when I heard the roar up ahead." Holing across the green, Watson had finished with a birdie. "From leading by two, I suddenly realised I had to par the last to tie," says Newton. "There really shouldn't have been a play-off."

Though it seems preposterous now, Watson had arrived at Carnoustie with a reputation as a choker after squandering both the 1974 and 1975 US Opens. The Press would doubtless hammer him again if he didn't produce the goods this time, but the experience of being in contention over the weekend had hardened Watson, who scrambled his way around Carnoustie to make sure of his maiden victory, ultimately outscoring Newton 71-72.

Minutes before the play-off Newton had been told that Watson was a suspect putter—"the sort of tip I usually get down at the racetrack" laments the Australian—but time and time again he holed the putts that mattered. Starting that week at Carnoustie, Watson was unquestionably the best pressure-putter in the business, and for a decade would be the dominant player in world golf. That this was Carnoustie elevated the 25-year-old into the company of such luminaries as Tommy Armour, Henry Cotton, Ben Hogan and Gary Player, all previous winners there.

"Great players make things happen," says Newton, generously recollecting the events of that afternoon. "Looking back on the play-off, Tom played great shots from difficult positions at the crucial times. At the par-3 eighth he hooked his tee shot beneath the wire fence left of the green. He had to play a shot where he took the club between the strands of wire, and he needed a lot of strength in the arms to get the ball up over the bunker and on the green, whereupon he holed the putt from 25 feet for a par. No normal player would do that. I was one shot in front playing the 14th, and he holes a sand wedge for eagle. Down the years he has become known for making this type of impossible shot, retrieving seemingly hopeless situations."

In a perfect world, this story of Tom and Jack would have been the first of many classic encounters, one in a series of memorable cameos in parallel careers. The reality is that while the 25-year-old from Kansas City would go on from Carnoustie to become one of the game's greatest players, with a haul of Open titles matched only by J.H. Taylor, James Braid and Peter Thomson, and bettered only by Harry Vardon, the Australian's career would sparkle only intermittently before being extinguished altogether in the most horrifying fashion.

On 24 July 1983, barely a week after Watson had pocketed that fifth Open at Royal Birkdale, then 33 years old and in the prime of his life, Newton walked into a whirling propeller blade and out of professional golf forever. Seven and a half hours on the operating table saved his life, but he lost his right arm and right eye. There have been numerous sur-

Carnoustie was longer and tougher than Watson remembered it to be, and he missed the 36-hole cut by one stroke.

geries since, and not a day goes by that Newton does not feel the pain or remember the fight. "But I couldn't let go, I guess," Newton says. "My girl, Christie, was only 5, my boy, Clint, just 2. I didn't want to see them grow up without a father. They were too young. So was I."

Given that we are talking about an Aussie, and a man to whom the gift of life far outweighs anything in golf, it is not in the least bit surprising to hear Newton talk matter-of-factly about his experience and the way in which he has since rebuilt his life. "I'm not bitter at all," he says, "I'm by nature a positive person. I don't dwelt on the past and what I don't have. I think of what I do have."

As the chairman of the Australasian PGA Tour, a respected writer and accomplished broadcaster, he doesn't have the time to live in the past. After the accident, the Australian prime minister, Bob Hawke, asked Newton to set up a national junior golf pro-

gramme, a task to which he has taken with relish. "The problem with golf is that it tends to sit on its backside and not promote itself among young people," he says, feisty as he ever was. "I've set out to get more kids playing golf, not necessarily searching out a champion, just getting them out to enjoy themselves. The kids are the future."

Just the wrong side of the cut, a shot off the mark, Watson's participation at golf's greatest championship was over for another year. Newton would be there for the weekend, commentating for Australia's 7 Network, his personal experiences in golf and in life providing a rare and profound sense of perspective. "If I could stick my arm back on I'd just love to get out there and play," he says, nodding first at his empty jacket sleeve before gazing out across the links. "No matter how a course is set up, my philosophy is that you bring your golf clubs to a tournament and you let them do the talking."

Jesper Parnevik (145) signalled a successful finish at level-par 71 to be amongst the contenders at the half-way stage.

PAR FALLS TO DIVERSE FIELD

BY ANDY FARRELL

Where no one ventured the previous day, seven players made it in the second round of the Open. They walked out of the new hotel and onto the first tee, and by the time they walked off the 18th green and back into the safety of the hotel they may have been wearied by the almost five hours of concentration but were joyful at having secured sub-par rounds at Carnoustie.

After the first round, statisticians noted that the lowest number of rounds under 70 in any Open was two, on five occasions, the last in the Open at Carnoustie in 1968. The possibility of setting a new record, or adding to the list, was swiftly dashed.

Four players managed rounds in the 60s, led by France's Jean Van de Velde with 68 that gave him the halfway lead at 143, one over par. There were 69s for David Frost and Costantino Rocca, both of whom had failed to break 80 on Thursday, and for Argentina's Angel Cabrera, who moved into second place at 144, two over.

Three others scored rounds of 70, Mark Brooks, with the day's lowest first nine of 32 thanks to birdies at four of the first six holes, Tim Herron and Greg Norman.

The leaderboard now had an international flavour with a Frenchman leading from an Argentinean, with Jesper Parnevik of Sweden one further back at 145 and an Australian, an American and another Swede sharing fourth place at 146 in the form of Norman, Tiger Woods and Patrik Sjoland.

To tame the beast of Carnoustie, it seemed, it helped to be a bit of an animal yourself. There was Tiger and the Shark and also Cabrera, whose nickname at home in Cordoba is "El Pato," or "the Duck." And Van de Velde has more than a passing acquaintance with a certain Donald Duck as he is sponsored by Disneyland Paris.

Once again the wind blew hard, but the early morning calm lasted longer than the previous day. All seven of the sub-par men had early starting times, but Van de Velde was actually the last of them to set off, at 10.25. He therefore played most of his round in similar conditions to the day before, but managed to score seven strokes better.

It helped that for 12 holes he did not drop a shot. Better than that, he birdied the sixth, with a putt from 30 feet, and the seventh, with a four iron to 15 feet. He bogeyed the 13th and failed to birdie the par-5 14th, one of only two holes to average under its par. Now he stood on the 15th tee, and his thoughts returned to how he played the last four holes in the first round.

"Playing the 15th yesterday, I was level par," he recalled. "But then I put an iron into the bunker on 15 and had to chip out sideways because it hit the face and plugged. Then I hit a seven iron to six feet and missed. So I bogeyed there and I bogeyed 16 because again I missed the green and didn't get up and down. Then on 17 I made a perfect drive but took a wrong decision. I took a two iron, tried to hit it low and ended in the face of a bunker. So that was a 6 but, you know, 75 was still all right, no disaster, just a poor finish."

This time, leaving the 14th green, Van de Velde turned to his caddie, a compatriot by the name of Christophe Angiolini, and said, "I will try to think well, try to hit the proper shots and let's try to put four pars in the bag." He confirmed later, "I wanted to do better than the first round." He did.

Through the back of the 15th green, after a four iron and an eight iron, he chipped to three feet to get up and down. At the next, the 250-yard 16th, he found the green and holed across the putting surface, fully 50 feet, "a monster," he enthused, for a birdie 2. At 17, he safely took his par, and then at the last, a 487-yard hole playing downwind, he hit a two iron

Jean Van de Velde (143) returned with 68 after a 50-foot birdie putt on the 16th and a wedge to three feet at the last.

Angel Cabrera (144) had 69 but thought he had made bogey at the 18th...

and a wedge to three feet for another birdie. From four over the previous day, he was two under for the last four holes this time. No one else got close to doing the same.

"Obviously, I am very pleased," Van de Velde said. "It is very, very tough. If you miss a fairway, you are not going to get a break, you just have to go out sideways. And it is very draining to be out there all day. The holes playing downwind are at least as difficult as those into the wind, probably more because you have to allow for the run and the bounce."

No Frenchman had won the Open since Arnaud Massy at Hoylake in 1907, and Van de Velde was the first from his country to be leading since Jean Garaialde tied with Christy O'Connor Snr after the first round at St Andrews in 1964.

"Garaialde was certainly a source of inspiration, but so were Nicklaus and Watson and also Ballesteros," Van de Velde said. "I went to see Seve play in the French Open and on many occasions, but there were not many French players chancing their luck at the international level until people like Emmanuel Dussart went on tour in the mid 1980s."

For Cabrera, there was the inspiration of Roberto de Vicenzo winning the Open in 1967, also at Hoy-

...until the wind pushed his ball into the hole.

Despite triple bogey at the 17th, Greg Norman (146) finished with 70 to be three strokes off the lead.

Costantino Rocca (150) improved from 81 to 69.

lake. Eduardo Romero, "El Gato" or "The Cat," from Cordoba as well, also provided a role model and, indeed, financial help before Cabrera got through the qualifying tournament for the PGA European Tour at the fourth attempt in 1995. "We are still very good friends," Cabrera said through an interpreter, "and the thing Eduardo always tells me is, 'Behave yourself on the course.'"

Having finished runner-up to Sergio Garcia in the Murphy's Irish Open two weeks before, Cabrera was in fine form and when he hit a seven iron to two feet at the 16th, he claimed his fourth birdie of the round. "The big names don't matter to me," he added. "All I see is the course. I don't know who is behind me."

Almost everyone, actually, but it was Norman who was beginning to look a potent threat. Since his narrow defeat by Jose Maria Olazabal at the Masters, the Australian had not played a lot of golf and, at the age of 44, his warm-up for his 21st appearance in the Open was to play with his son Gregory at courses like Royal Dornoch rather than any competitive action.

Strangely, just before he was due to leave for Britain, Norman's clubs were stolen by a workman mend-

Brian Watts (147) said, "If you don't drive it on the fairway, you can't play this golf course."

ing his roof at home in Florida, but the clubs were soon recovered.

Starting the day five over par, Norman birdied the fourth from 25 feet to go out in 35. A putt of similar distance then gave him the first of three birdies in a row at the 12th. A pitching wedge to 12 inches set up a 2 at the short 13th and he two-putted from long range at the next. While Rocca had gone on to make it four birdies in a row at the 15th, Norman returned to his par-making and was still four under for the round on the 17th tee.

Given a par at the last was to follow, the 17th, 459 yards into the wind and now the hardest hole on the course, was Norman's only other deviation from par. It cost the Shark a triple-bogey 7.

His drive finished three yards off the fairway, but so thick was the rough he did not move the ball as he attempted to hack out. On his next swing, Norman got the ball over the Barry Burn into the rough on the left. From there he had to chop out again and, from the fairway, was short with his fifth before getting up and down for the triple bogey.

"I got a real dose of the punishment and it doesn't feel good," admitted the two-times Open champion.

Patrik Sjoland (146) birdied two of the last four for 72.

Ian Woosnam (150), with 74, had four birdies.

"I don't think my tee shot deserved or warranted having an air swing for my second shot. I was right over the top of it and couldn't see the ball. I had to guesstimate where it was and was only trying to move it six, 12 feet, not 100 yards.

"I don't think that's the way the game should be played. The width of the fairway is fine, but not having rough you cannot move your ball in nine feet off the fairway. I don't like the circumstances I got the 7, but I accept it. Forgetting that hole, I did what I wanted to do today and got myself into position come the weekend."

Woods was doing exactly the same, and still managing to do what he wanted in keeping a high number off his card. His 72 promised more than it delivered after he rolled in a 30-footer at the first and again he had a poor finish, bogeying the 16th and 18th.

"Right now good shots are borderline," Woods said. "You have to hit great shots. But I have always enjoyed playing in terrible conditions. Growing up in southern California, we didn't have too many bad days but I took advantage of the ones we did have because I enjoyed it. You have to use your repertoire of shots and not be afraid to trust your instincts. I'm in good shape right now. Any time you are moving up spots on the leaderboard, you must be playing well."

The American was suffering from hayfever, but not as severely as Parnevik, whose level-par 71 in the circumstances might have been the most valiant effort of the day. "It could have been 78 or 79, so to shoot 71 is beyond my dreams, actually," said the Swede. "I was very close to walking in after the fifth. I was sneezing constantly and my nose was dripping all the time, even on the ball. I had to time my putts and shots between the sneezes."

Parnevik stuck a bit of tissue up each nostril and a marshal came to his aid by seeking medical assistance. "He gave me something that was going to help but it didn't, actually," Parnevik said. "But then I birdied No 7, so I decided to carry on."

There, he hit one of his best one irons to 20 feet and holed the putt, while at the next, the 183-yard eighth hole, he hit a seven iron to six feet. Playing in

Tiger Woods (146) was two over par for the championship after this birdie on the 14th.

Justin Leonard (147) returned with 74, saying, "I just hung in there because I didn't play that well."

Korean Kyoung-ju Choi (148) had a round of 72.

difficult conditions appealed to Parnevik's enquiring mind and sense of the ridiculous, and he had twice been a runner-up in the Open, at Turnberry in 1994 and at Royal Troon in 1997.

"At the eighth, I was just trying to hook it at the out of bounds on the left and hoping the wind was going to straighten it out sooner or later," he said.

His second nine consisted of a birdie at the 10th and a bogey at the 17th to be two behind Van de Velde.

After 36 holes, Justin Leonard and Paul Lawrie were four behind at five over par after both had rounds of 74. If neither man took full advantage of the slightly easier conditions in the morning, both showed the virtue of not giving up.

Colin Montgomerie had 76 that left him at eight over par, despite the fact he was out in the fourth group of the day. Distractions such as photographers and television cameramen seemed to claim most of his attention during the round.

"It wasn't a difficult day," Monty said. "I had a great draw and didn't capitalise on it. I'm afraid it's gone now. I'm just looking forward to Medinah." This was a reference to the forthcoming USPGA Championship.

After 79 on the opening day, David Duval im-

Paul Lawrie (147) was putting his skills around the greens to good use, posting scores of 73 and 74.

Davis Love III (148) took double bogey on the eighth.

Bradley Hughes (147) had a level-par 71.

Caddie Jerry Higginbotham (left) and his man, young Sergio Garcia (172), were alone at the bottom of the standings.

proved to 75 with both a double-bogey 7 at the sixth and an eagle 3 at the 14th. The American had found himself in difficulty with some sections of the Press concerning his apparent disenchantment with the course. "I don't dislike the golf course and I don't believe I said I did and, if I did, I was mistaken because I don't," he attempted to clarify. He went on, "I just think it is really, really tough right now. You can't judge your game on this course. Good shots end up in the hay, bad shots end up on the green."

At 12 over par, Duval made the 36-hole cut right on the qualifying mark. The list of notable names who didn't make it was long, but one name not expected to be leaving so soon was that of Rodney Pampling. Never before had the first-round leader in the Open missed the cut. He did so with 86, one of the 31 rounds of 80 or worse during the day. He had 10 bogeys, a double bogey and a triple bogey.

"I didn't feel worried being the leader," said the Australian. "I just got off to a slow start with bogeys at the first two holes and you can't pick it up on this course. I didn't play well all day and kept getting bad lies. All of a sudden, you have a lot of score. I will always have the knowledge that I led the Open, but I will always have the bad second round, too."

Mark O'Meara improved from 83 to 74 but became the first defending champion since Mark Calcavecchia in 1990 to miss the cut. On the same 15-over-par score was Olazabal, the Masters champion who broke his hand punching a wall during the US Open, and Nick Faldo. Having made his debut in the Open in 1976 at the age of 18, the three-times champion was playing in his 24th Open and this was his first missed cut. He would not be around to celebrate his 42nd birthday on the final day.

Others to miss out were Phil Mickelson, the runner-up at the US Open but who had not played since due to the birth of his baby daughter, and former champions Calcavecchia, Tom Watson, Tom Lehman, Seve Ballesteros, Sandy Lyle, Tony Jacklin, Gary Player and Bob Charles. Watson came home in 32, the best inward half of the day, only to miss out by one stroke.

It was a dignified exit for the 1975 champion. Not so for Sergio Garcia. The Spanish wonder kid showed his youthfulness with 83 to finish dead last at 30 over par. He went home with his family but said that for the first time in 10 years, he would not be watching the Open on television. He had had enough.

Jose Maria Olazabal (157) went home after 36 holes.

Phil Mickelson (155) was out by one stroke.

Vijay Singh (161) posted scores of 77 and 84.

Nick Faldo (157) missed his first Open cut.

SECOND ROUND RESULTS

HOLE	1	2	3	4	5	6	7	8	9	10	11	12	13	14	15	16	17	18	
PAR	4	4	4	4	4	5	4	3	4	4	4	4	3	5	4	3	4	4	TOTAL
Jean Van de Velde	4	4	4	4	4	4	3	3	4	4	4	4	4	5	4	2	4	3	68-143
Angel Cabrera	4	3	4	4	4	6	4	2	4	4	4	4	3	4	4	2	5	4	69-144
Jesper Parnevik	4	4	4	5	4	6	3	2	4	3	4	4	3	5	4	3	5	4	71-145
Patrik Sjoland	4	4	4	4	4	5	5	3	5	3	4	6	3	4	4	2	4	4	72-146
Greg Norman	4	4	4	3	4	5	4	3	4	4	4	3	2	4	4	3	7	4	70-146
Tiger Woods	3	4	4	4	3	5	5	2	4	4	5	5	3	4	4	4	4	5	72-146
Brian Watts	4	6	4	4	4	5	4	4	4	3	4	5	3	4	4	4	4	3	73-147
Bradley Hughes	3	4	4	4	4	4	4	4	4	4	5	4	2	5	4	3	4	5	71-147
Justin Leonard	4	4	4	4	4	5	5	3	5	5	4	5	2	4	4	4	4	4	74-147
Len Mattiace	5	5	4	4	5	5	4	3	6	4	4	4	3	3	3	3	6	3	74-147
Paul Lawrie	4	5	4	5	4	5	4	3	4	3	4	5	4	4	4	3	5	4	74-147
Kyoung-ju Choi	4	4	4	4	5	6	3	4	3	3	3	4	3	4	4	3	4	5	72-148
Davis Love III	4	5	4	3	4	5	3	5	4	4	5	4	2	6	4	3	5	4	74-148
Andrew Coltart	4	3	3	4	4	6	5	4	4	4	4	5	3	4	4	3	5	5	74-148
David Frost	4	4	3	4	4	5	4	4	4	4	4	4	3	4	4	3	4	3	69-149
Jim Furyk	4	4	4	3	4	5	4	3	4	4	4	5	2	4	5	3	4	5	71-149
Bernhard Langer	4	4	4	3	5	5	5	4	4	5	4	4	3	4	5	4	5	5	77-149
Steve Pate	4	5	5	3	3	9	5	3	4	4	4	4	3	5	4	3	4	4	76-149
Scott Dunlap	5	3	5	3	4	5	5	4	5	4	5	4	3	4	4	5	5	4	77-149
Katsuyoshi Tomori	4	4	4	5	4	5	4	4	5	4	4	4	3	4	4	4	5	4	75-149

HOLE SUMMARY

HOLE	PAR	EAGLES	BIRDIES	PARS	BOGEYS	HIGHER	RANK	AVERAGE
1	4	0	12	87	49	6	12	4.32
2	4	0	12	79	50	13	8	4.42
3	4	0	26	106	21	1	17	3.98
4	4	0	14	85	47	8	11	4.33
5	4	0	12	100	35	7	15	4.24
6	5	0	9	67	61	17	3	5.60
7	4	0	11	64	67	12	5	4.53
8	3	0	14	94	39	7	13	3.27
9	4	0	6	74	61	13	4	4.55
OUT	36	0	116	756	430	84		39.23
10	4	0	21	82	43	8	14	4.25
11	4	0	5	95	45	9	10	4.38
12	4	0	3	70	67	14	2	4.62
13	3	0	26	98	30	0	16	3.03
14	5	5	78	60	10	1	18	4.51
15	4	0	10	80	54	10	8	4.42
16	3	0	9	76	62	7	6	3.44
17	4	0	6	66	61	21	1	4.66
18	4	0	14	74	52	14	6	4.44
IN	35	5	172	701	424	84		37.73
TOTAL	71	5	288	1457	854	168		76.96

Players Below Par	7		**LOW SCORES**	
Players At Par	6	Low First Nine	Mark Brooks	32
Players Above Par	141	Low Second Nine	Tom Watson	32
		Low Round	Jean Van de Velde	68

WEATHER

Temperature: low 12°C, high 22°C.
Strong southwest breeze.

The Caledonia Kettle dates back to 1901 and goes to the winner of The Annual Club Championship

Spanish sensation Sergio Garcia was last amongst those completing 36 holes, with scores of 89 and 83.

NO MATCH FOR THE COURSE

BY RON SIRAK

Among the complex components that make up genius is the ability to knock down the walls of preconception and see the world with fresh eyes. And just as surely, on a more mundane level, sometimes the simple art of survival draws heavily on an ability to adapt to unfamiliarity. Even as the week of the 128th Open Championship dawned, it became clear that this would not be a time of genius on the Carnoustie Golf Links, but one of survival. And the fittest who would survive this extreme test would be not the physically strong, but the mentally agile.

There has perhaps never been a major championship in which so many players were eliminated before the first ball was struck in anger. Carnoustie, it was clear early on, would be a mind game and it was just as clear early on which of the competitors had already been worn down by the devilishly difficult set-up conspired to by the Championship Committee of the Royal and Ancient Golf Club and the outspoken and enthusiastic greenkeeper, John Philp.

"Like a lot of things in life, golf has gone soft," Philp said while sitting beneath a photo of Ben Hogan in his cluttered office at the maintenance shed near the 10th green. "It's about character and how it stands up to adversity. Sorry, but that's my opinion. Golf is a character builder."

All that was needed was to listen to the self doubts of the players to know that there was much truth in what Philp said. And as the championship commenced, he found not so much a resolve among players to figure out a way to handle the Carnoustie design, but more a resignation among many that they were no match for the links. The cries reverberated from the newly constructed hotel all the way to the North Sea.

"The fairways are too narrow," they moaned. "The rough is too high," they whinged. "The course is too long," they sighed. "The wind and unfortunate bounces that turned good shots into bad and bad shots into miserable are unfair," they groaned.

The gloomy warnings were issued early on and, unfortunately for them, those players who became obsessed with criticising the course rather than trying to figure out how to play it all but eliminated themselves from the competition.

"Of all the Open Championships I've played in, I think this is by far the toughest set-up I've ever seen," defending champion Mark O'Meara, who was playing in the Open for the 15th time, said on the eve of the championship. "Not only is the rough extremely deep and very difficult to play out of, but the golf course is very narrow, too. Throw the wind on top of that, with the length of this golf course, it's going to be a heck of a contest just to try and make pars. I think the person who stays patient and remains calm will win. How are they going to adapt?"

The calm perspective offered by the veteran O'Meara was lost on many in the field. While the complaints and fears about Carnoustie were expressed in many different languages in this most international of golfing events, the loudest and most persistent wails were carried in the unmistakable English spoken by Americans. Perhaps the loudest complaint about the course set-up was expressed in the deafening body language of David Duval, who on Wednesday seemed to be crying out with every muscle, "Get me out of here." Certainly, he put as little effort into his attempt to disguise his displeasure as he did in his efforts to articulate it.

Asked if Carnoustie was set up too hard for the championship, Duval said, "I can't define too hard, too easy, unfair, fair. So it is what it is." Asked to describe what it is, Duval said, "You tell me." Then after a few more grunts and winces, he added, "It looks to me like we are playing an event based on target golf on a links layout."

David Duval was one of the critics.

The point seemingly lost to those who complained the most was the simple fact that the sole purpose of a golf tournament is not to compete against a rather arbitrary notion of par, but rather to compete against the others in the field and to try to post the lowest score.

"Too difficult?" Sir Michael Bonallack, Secretary of the R and A, said, repeating the most-asked question of the week. "I think it is fair. When Hogan played here there was no such thing as par. You didn't give scores in relation to par at all. It is only a fairly recent thing."

Philp was not only an advocate of that perspective on golf, but as greenkeeper was in position to make Carnoustie reflect that philosophy. "I don't go too much on actual scoring," Philp said. "Over and under par is a wee bit secondary. It's about the challenge and what God has given you."

While Duval became the point man for the dissident faction at Carnoustie, he was nowhere near alone. But seemingly lost in the moaning was the simple fact that everyone was playing the same golf course under the same conditions. At times the situation almost begged for someone to cry out, "Quit complaining and play golf."

But what should not be lost on anyone paying even the slightest bit of attention was that the leaderboard produced by Carnoustie going into the weekend was composed of those players best able to revise their expectations. Jean Van de Velde, Justin Leonard and Paul Lawrie know all about grinding. They are not players who ever expect to overwhelm a golf course.

Greg Norman, as he was at the Masters, once again showing he can still contend in a major championship, might be the definition of resilience in golf. Who has bounced back from more disappointments? And Tiger Woods emerged at Carnoustie as a maturer, more composed and more complete player than ever before, one clearly excited by the challenge of trying to adapt to difficult conditions.

This was a major championship where egos needed to be checked at the door. Those players unable to do that lost their focus, lost their concentration and lost their chance at success.

"It's John's philosophy to make the players think," assistant greenkeeper Angus McRae said about Philp, his boss. "Why set the course up in the way the players want it so they can shoot 20 under par? Some of the scores in tournaments are getting ridiculous."

By the time 36 holes were in the books, an astonishing array of big-name players were found lacking in the ability to make the mental adjustment to playing Carnoustie. Phil Mickelson, Tom Lehman, Masters champion Jose Maria Olazabal, defending champion O'Meara, Steve Elkington, Vijay Singh and Nick Faldo—for the first time in 24 Opens—all missed the cut. The wonder kid Sergio Garcia was dead last.

"You can't judge your game on this golf course," Duval said Friday after playing the final four holes five over par and making the 36-hole cut right at the number at 12 over par. "Good shots end up in the hay, bad shots end up on the green." When Ernie Els was asked following the second round if he had ever experienced anything like the difficulty of Carnoustie before, he shrugged, looked at the ground and then at the sky, as if seeking out a heavenly answer, before saying, "I'm getting tired of that question."

If there is a lesson that touring professional and recreational golfer alike should take away from Carnoustie, it is that golf is a constant series of mental adjustments. And the more a player becomes distracted by bad breaks or unfair conditions or high scoring, the more likely he is to fail.

"I've never played the course this severe, but you've just got to get on with it," said Lawrie midway through the championship. "The course is there, the same for everyone and you've just got to go on and do your job." It was definitely a winning attitude.

In a more economical, but no less articulate use of English, Van de Velde said, "It is tough, that's all. It is very, very tough."

Why did so many players lose perspective and allow Carnoustie to get inside their heads at the Open? Maybe Philp was correct in saying they have grown soft because they do not face adversity as often as players from another era. In the quiet words of the few who managed to capture the spirit of Carnoustie were the pearls of wisdom needed to compete in the severest of Open Championships.

"There's a lot of good players being blown away today," Montgomerie said after the first round. "I think it was a day more for courage than for skill." A day later, Leonard chimed in with the assessment that the challenge was "more mental than it is physical." Five-times Open champion Tom Watson shot 32 on the second nine on Friday—proving that scoring was possible—and missed the cut by one stroke. He offered this insight: "Bobby Jones said golf was not meant to be a fair game."

Somehow, that essential point was lost on many. And, strangely, it was a player as young as 23-year-old Woods—not always the model of composure on the golf course—who was among those who grasped it the best.

"Was it fair?" Woods asked. "Um, it's great that we all had to play in it." Woods described the play as the most gruelling competition he had ever participated in. "Are we even close to being done?" he asked his caddie, Steve Williams, on the 11th hole Friday. "It's just the mental drain of having to stay in on every shot, because there's really no shot you can relax on."

While no one would ever even begin to say that the conditions produced at Carnoustie were fun, there were those who understood that a certain pleasure can be obtained in figuring out how to handle adver-

John Philp said, "Golf has gone soft."

sity. It was the absolutely necessary key to survival.

"If you don't enjoy it, it's going to grab and bite you hard," Mark McNulty said.

"You've got to never give up," Davis Love III said. "There were a couple of times today when I could have snapped and lost it, but I hung in there."

That was an attitude sorely lacking at Carnoustie. And perhaps there was a sweet symmetry in the fact that the seemingly random nature of the game that Philp tried so hard to bring out in his course's set-up proved to be the most frustrating to many players.

"I know there is a bit of lottery in the way this course plays," Philp said. "They want to eliminate that element of luck. The top players take badly with the bad bounces. That is critical. The element of luck is absolutely critical. You take that away and you don't have the real game of golf."

Then, with a pause and a glance back at the photo of Hogan that overlooks his desk, Philp said, "I tried to retain typical links character and provide a challenge to the modern, stronger player with better equipment. They have psychologists and titanium, all I have is what God gave me—nature."

And left unsaid between the lines was the clear attitude in Philp that were Hogan at Carnoustie for the 128th Open, he would have figured out a way to play the tough old course, and that he would have done it in silence, without a whimper of complaint.

Jean Van de Velde (213) birdied two of the last four holes for 70 to open a five-stroke lead going to the final round.

IT'S FIVE SHOTS, BY JEAN

BY ANDY FARRELL

Willie Milne had just 40 minutes' notice that he was required to act as a marker in the third round of the Open Championship. Martyn Thompson, a club professional from Dorset, was the odd man out in the day's first tee time. He scored 78. Milne, a former Walker Cup player, had recently taken over as professional at the new Carnoustie Golf Hotel. He knows a thing or two about links golf.

Albeit without the pressure of actually competing in the Open, Milne returned 76. "I don't know what they are all complaining about," Milne said with a wry smile. "It wasn't that difficult."

Perhaps the only man actually playing in the Open who could share that view was Jean Van de Velde. The Frenchman started the day leading by one stroke and, with a third round of 70, completed 54 holes with a 213 total and a five-stroke advantage.

The previous day, Van de Velde said one of the heroes who inspired him to play the game was Seve Ballesteros. On this Saturday, he played like Seve. He got up and down from everywhere, holed everything, it seemed, on the greens. Just when the rest of the field thought he was heading back towards them, Van de Velde birdied the 14th and the 18th, the latter accompanied with an impassioned fist-pumping display, to lay down a comfortable cushion for the night. He was the only player to stand at level par for the championship with one round to play.

A calm but drizzly start gave way to the strongest gusts of the week around lunchtime and early afternoon, before the wind died again and the sun came out to shepherd the Frenchman home. Only three men, out of the 73 who had qualified for the last two rounds, broke par. Van de Velde's 70 was matched by Frank Nobilo, which took the New Zealander from 10 to nine over par.

The low round of the day, compiled in the worst of the weather, was by Craig Parry. The Australian's 67 reduced by one Van de Velde's low round of the week and left Parry sharing second place at 218 with Justin Leonard. The American, who like David Frost scored a level-par 71, was a familiar figure to be five strokes off the lead, the margin he made up to win at Royal Troon in 1997, as well as on two other occasions.

Andrew Coltart, with 72, shared fourth place at 220 with Frost and Tiger Woods, who was birdieless in his 74. Greg Norman, after his 75, and Angel Cabrera, following his 77 playing with Van de Velde in the last pairing, were one stroke further back at 221. Five players were at 222. They were Nobilo, Colin Montgomerie, Bernhard Langer, Len Mattiace and Miguel Angel Martin. At 223 lurked Hal Sutton, Paul Lawrie, Patrik Sjoland and Jesper Parnevik. The two Swedes had played together in the penultimate pairing but fell back with scores of 77 and 78.

Van de Velde, leading a major championship for the first time, might have been expected to be the one to slip away. Yet no one in the last four twoballs came within four strokes of his 70. Instead, the biggest move of the day came from Parry. The diminutive Aussie started in a tie for 30th place at 151 and continued to make progress up the leaderboard even after completing his round. "You know, I am actually only five-foot-six, but I felt six-foot out there the way I was playing," he said.

Parry finished third in the Scottish Open at Carnoustie in 1995 and had led the fairways hit statistic at the US Open last month at Pinehurst. "That shows you how I was hitting my driver and I was always looking forward to coming here," he said.

For the first two days, Parry had kept out of the spotlight playing alongside Woods and Ian Woosnam. "I was a little disappointed the way I played in the first two rounds," he said. "I played terribly the first day. Playing with Tiger and Woosie, I was just

Craig Parry (218) scored six birdies in a round of 67 to advance into a tie for second place.

trying to hang in there. They probably dragged me up to their level. I couldn't get anything going. Lo and behold, today I got off to a good start."

Parry birdied the third from six feet and felt he might be in for a good day when he holed from 35 feet from off the front of the green at the fourth. At the par-5 sixth, he put a one iron into the rough but had a good enough lie to hit a seven iron up the fairway. With 224 yards to the flag, he then hit another one iron to six feet and holed that for his third birdie. His fourth birdie came courtesy of a 15-footer at the 10th, but he immediately three-putted for bogey at the next.

The dropped shot did not affect his momentum. He got up and down from a bunker at the 14th for another birdie and then hit a five iron to 12 feet for birdie at the 16th. "I am always happy to hit that green, let alone make birdie," Parry said. He could not get up and down from a thick patch of rough by the 17th green, but was still delighted by his effort.

"I feel I am in a great position to have a run at the championship. It is what everyone dreams of," Parry said. Never as successful in America as his record at home and in Europe suggests he could be, the 32-year-old Parry led going into the final round of the 1992 US Masters but collapsed with a final round of 78. "The Masters was a long time ago," he said. "I was a little bit young.

"A lot of guys are complaining about this course," he added, "but someone is going to walk away with their name on the trophy. There is no use complaining about it. I've done enough of that about our courses in Australia, and it is only going to get you into trouble. I really like bouncing the ball into the aprons of these greens. You have to use the banks and things like that. You've got to know links golf. I think I've had a long enough apprenticeship of playing links golf."

Other players had soon taken note of Parry's advance. "I did find myself watching the leaderboard to gauge what was going on," said Leonard. "Craig Parry's 67 is an incredible score, but for the most part, par is a very good score too. Basically, the way I have tried to play all week is to play fairly conserva-

David Frost (220) posted 71 to tie for fourth place.

tively, and that didn't change too much today. I've accomplished my primary goal at the beginning of the week of having a chance to win the tournament going into Sunday."

When Leonard won at Royal Troon in 1997, his family had watched on television back home in Dallas. This time, his father Larry was on the trip but decided Saturday was the day to sneak over to play at Gleneagles. "Last night," Justin reported, "he was asking if it was okay for him to go play and I said: 'You can't bring your golf clubs over here and not play once.'"

Leonard's round was up and down—three birdies and a bogey on the first nine, three bogeys and a birdie on the second nine—but this was steadiness itself compared to Van de Velde.

Van de Velde missed the green on the left at the second and dropped a shot, but got it straight back with a birdie at the next. At the fourth his drive finished in the rough and he had to chip out sideways before hitting a seven iron to 20 feet. His putt for par

Tiger Woods (220) scored 74 with bogey from the rough on the seventh and later double bogey on the 17th.

Angel Cabrera (221) had 77 to fall behind.

just missed, and he was back to one over par again.

But at the seventh, Van de Velde holed from 25 feet and made it to the turn in level par for the day. Here was where the fun and games started. From the 10th tee, Van de Velde drove into a bunker on the left. The lie was not good so he decided to lay up short of the Barry Burn. From 95 yards, his wedge approach stopped 15 feet from the hole and he sunk the putt. "So that was a big relief," he said.

Another poor drive at the 11th finished in what can be described as jungle to the right of the fairway. Van de Velde lingered on the tee about to play a provisional, but "I could see someone's hand waving just over the top of the grass, so I thought he had it." That was not the end of his problems.

Given such an awful lie, Van de Velde decided his only option, instead of going for the green, was to chip sideways onto the fairway. For this shot, however, there was a television camera tower in his line of sight. "I asked the referee if I could get relief or, if I played it, if I killed the cameraman, what would happen?" Van de Velde explained. "The only shot I had was to come back on the fairway."

Justin Leonard (218) had 71 after he went out in 34, two under, then made three bogeys on the second nine.

Van de Velde had a magical day around the greens, concluding with this 45-foot putt for birdie.

He acknowledged the applause after his 70, one under par.

The referee with his group, Michael Lunt, granted free relief from the tower, although this was later admitted to be a mistake. From the fairway, Van de Velde pitched to six feet and holed the putt for another extraordinary par.

Having followed the instructions of the referee, Van de Velde was not liable for the error. Later, David Rickman, the R and A Rules Secretary, reviewed the television coverage and explained, "It is regrettable that the ruling on the 11th hole with Jean Van de Velde was incorrect. In the circumstances, the player's request was both reasonable and understandable, but, in accordance with the Local Rule for Temporary Immovable Obstructions, relief should not have been granted because no part of the tower intervened between the player's ball and the hole. That having been said, the referee's decision is final (Rule 34-2)."

At the time, Van de Velde had a bigger worry about his driving. At the 12th, he found another bunker off the tee. He was short of the green in two and missed a 12-footer for par. Had his luck come to an end? At the short 13th, his tee shot hit the flag. It could have dropped into the hole, but it bounced off

Frank Nobilo (222) shared ninth place.

six feet away and he missed the birdie chance.

Perhaps he felt hard done by when, with a three wood this time, he found another bunker off the 14th tee. He came out short of the Spectacles bunkers and put his third onto the adjoining fourth green at the back of the 14th. He was 70 feet away from the right hole, but, magically, the ball disappeared for a birdie. "A good bonus, yeah," he admitted.

Once again, Van de Velde stood on the 15th tee hoping for four pars but knowing that disaster lurked on each hole. This time his second shot found a bunker to the left of the 15th green but he came out to five feet and saved par. He made a good two-putt par at the 16th, and then found the right greenside bunker with his approach at the 17th. Another brilliant escape left him only a tap-in for par. And the last he played simply enough, with a two iron and a nine iron to 45 feet—and one putt. "For sure, I didn't play so well today, but I was fighting very hard and that's all I can do," he said.

Now it was time to confront the fact that a player ranked 152nd in the world who had won the qualifying at Monifieth was now leading the Open by five

Andrew Coltart (220) bogeyed two of the last three holes.

Miguel Angel Martin (222) returned with 72, having only two bogeys plus one birdie.

Jesper Parnevik (223) shot 78, including 7 at the 11th hole.

strokes. The following day a Frenchman, whose only previous victory came at the Roma Masters in 1993, would be attempting to win the Open for the first time in 92 years, since Arnaud Massy won at Hoylake in 1907.

"Definitely, I am surprised to be five ahead," Van de Velde said. "But, no, I'm not surprised with myself. If you believe you can make it through, it might happen. If you don't believe, it will never happen. This is the biggest tournament ever in the world, but perhaps one of the smallest players is going to win.

"Normally, I am very, very tense. I'm an intense guy, but, you know, how many times is it going to happen in the lifetime of a golfer to be leading the Open by five, to tee off last in the Open? Not that often, no matter how good you are. The only thing I have to prove is to myself.

"If I were to win, it would be fantastic, a dream come true, that's for sure. It would be big for golf in France. Maybe they can have a bit of a dance on the Champs Elysees. Definitely, I can tell you I'm going to start thinking about it because my IQ is a little bit over 10, I think.

"But the bottom line is, no matter what, even if I

Greg Norman (221) saw his chances dwindle with his 75, including bogeys on the last two holes.

Lee Westwood (225) posted 74, his best score of the championship, after starting with 76 and 75.

Paul Lawrie (223) took 76 to be 10 strokes behind.

Colin Montgomerie (222) recovered with a round of 72.

shoot 90 tomorrow, I'm going to enjoy it. Maybe people will say, 'Oh, he blew it,' or whatever. Maybe I'm going to blow it. It's the first time I've ever been there. What do you expect? You know I am not the number one in the world. My knees are going to touch each other on the first tee tomorrow. But, let me tell you, I'm going to enjoy it."

While Van de Velde went off to enjoy his customary red wine over dinner, the world's No 1 player, Woods, was recalling how he felt before the final round of the 1997 US Masters. "Anyone who has a lead like that has got to sleep on it," Woods said. "You know, that's not easy to do. It wasn't exactly an easy night's sleep before I won the Masters, and I had a nine-shot lead."

Woods made more pars than anyone else on Saturday, 16 of them, but bogeyed the seventh and finally had his first double bogey of the week at the 17th,

the result of missing the fairway off the tee. He could not remember a round in a major championship as a professional when he had not made a birdie, something he knew he could not afford on the final day.

"You can't really be more aggressive, but I have to be more precise," Woods said. "I have to hit the ball closer and give myself more legitimate chances.

"I'm making a lot of putts right now, but most of them are for par. As for myself and a few other players who are right in the hunt, we need to play great rounds of golf. What Craig Parry did today, we are going to have to do tomorrow."

Those in the hunt now included once again Montgomerie, despite his comments of the previous day that he was out of it. "I was just trying to deflect attention yesterday," Monty said. A 72, which could have been better but for dropped shots at the 15th and 17th, left him nine strokes back, but hopeful.

Nick Price (224) had advanced after starting with 77.

Darren Clarke (227) never got in contention.

"Realistically, with weather like this, you could score 67 in the last round of the Open to win. So I could get to five over." And would five over have a realistic chance, he was asked. "Christ, yes," he said. He was right.

His fellow Scot, Lawrie, was one shot further back at 10 over par. His third round had been a slightly disappointing 76 in which he started bogey, bogey, birdie, bogey, par, bogey, bogey. He then had the day's longest run of pars, from the eighth to the 17th, before another bogey at the last. "I didn't play well today and five over was about right," he said.

"I'd imagine 10 over is a little too much out of the question. Van de Velde looks hard to beat, but the beast might roar again tomorrow. I'll be trying hard and if I could shoot like Parry did today, then I can get back into the picture, but realistically you have to think it's too far away."

If Lawrie was not ruling himself out he was not, like Woods, definitely ruling himself in. For all those chasing Van de Velde, Woods laid the ground rules. "Anyone who is 10 over par still has a shot at it," Woods declared. "If you can post a number early, you never know what can happen."

Bernhard Langer (222) recovered from a second-round 77.

THIRD ROUND RESULTS

HOLE	1	2	3	4	5	6	7	8	9	10	11	12	13	14	15	16	17	18	
PAR	4	4	4	4	4	5	4	3	4	4	4	4	3	5	4	3	4	4	TOTAL
Jean Van de Velde	4	5	3	5	4	5	3	3	4	4	4	5	3	4	4	3	4	3	70-213
Craig Parry	4	4	3	3	4	4	4	3	4	3	5	4	3	4	4	2	5	4	67-218
Justin Leonard	4	4	4	3	4	4	5	2	4	5	4	5	3	4	4	4	4	4	71-218
David Frost	4	4	3	4	4	6	5	2	4	5	4	5	3	4	3	3	4	4	71-220
Andrew Coltart	4	4	4	4	3	5	5	3	4	4	4	4	3	4	4	5	5	4	72-220
Tiger Woods	4	4	4	4	4	5	5	3	4	4	4	4	3	5	4	3	6	4	74-220
Greg Norman	3	5	5	4	4	4	5	3	4	5	4	5	3	4	4	3	5	5	75-221
Angel Cabrera	4	5	4	4	5	7	4	3	4	4	4	4	3	4	5	4	4	5	77-221
Frank Nobilo	4	4	4	4	3	5	4	2	5	5	4	4	2	4	4	3	5	4	70-222
Miguel Angel Martin	4	4	4	4	4	5	4	3	5	4	4	5	3	5	3	3	4	4	72-222
Colin Montgomerie	4	4	4	4	3	6	5	3	4	3	4	3	3	4	5	4	5	4	72-222
Bernhard Langer	5	4	4	4	4	5	4	2	5	5	4	4	3	4	5	3	4	4	73-222
Len Mattiace	4	4	6	5	5	5	5	2	4	5	4	4	3	4	4	3	4	4	75-222
Hal Sutton	4	4	4	4	4	6	4	2	5	4	4	4	2	5	4	3	4	5	72-223
Paul Lawrie	5	5	3	5	4	6	5	3	4	4	4	4	3	5	4	3	4	5	76-223
Patrik Sjoland	3	4	3	5	4	5	5	4	5	5	4	4	4	5	4	4	4	5	77-223
Jesper Parnevik	4	4	4	5	4	5	4	3	5	5	7	4	3	4	5	3	5	4	78-223

HOLE SUMMARY

HOLE	PAR	EAGLES	BIRDIES	PARS	BOGEYS	HIGHER	RANK	AVERAGE
1	4	0	4	48	18	3	12	4.29
2	4	0	4	46	20	3	11	4.30
3	4	1	14	51	6	1	17	3.89
4	4	0	4	37	24	8	3	4.51
5	4	0	9	47	14	3	14	4.15
6	5	0	6	43	17	7	7	5.36
7	4	0	2	35	29	7	2	4.56
8	3	0	13	46	14	0	15	3.01
9	4	0	7	33	26	7	4	4.47
OUT	36	1	63	386	168	39		38.54
10	4	0	3	44	24	2	7	4.36
11	4	0	4	49	18	2	13	4.26
12	4	0	0	46	22	5	5	4.44
13	3	0	10	58	5	0	16	2.93
14	5	1	43	29	0	0	18	4.38
15	4	0	5	41	21	6	6	4.41
16	3	0	1	48	23	1	9	3.33
17	4	0	1	37	26	9	1	4.62
18	4	0	6	45	15	7	9	4.33
IN	35	1	73	397	154	32		37.06
TOTAL	71	2	136	783	322	71		75.59

Players Below Par	3		
Players At Par	2		
Players Above Par	68		

LOW SCORES

Low First Nine	Craig Parry	33
Low Second Nine	Lee Westwood	33
Low Round	Craig Parry	67

WEATHER

Temperature: low 12°C, high 26°C.
Southwest breeze.

Jean Van de Velde appeared to be marching into Open Championship history after three rounds.

HIGH DRAMA ON THE LINKS

BY ALISTER NICOL

Long into the 21st century Jean Van de Velde will be remembered as the man who all but tamed the cruel beast of Carnoustie only to be chewed up and spat out disdainfully by the monster. It will be quite a burden to bear because less than 48 hours after his collapse French kids had christened a triple bogey a "Van de Velde."

The fun-loving Frenchman with a vibrant sense of humour was on the very threshold of golfing greatness when he led by three shots with one par-4 to play. Admittedly it was a tough par-4, perhaps the most daunting in championship golf. What ensued bordered on burlesque and is catalogued in detail elsewhere in this annual.

Before Van de Velde could put his foot in the door, so to speak, he put both feet in the Barry Burn, and his head under a figurative guillotine. He played the 72nd hole of the 128th Open Championship like a loose cannon careering around the deck of a Man O' War in a 19th century sea battle. His near-manic stare, his Gallic good looks, his "je ne c'est quoi" demeanour, made for great television. As did his theatrical, slow-motion stripping off of shoes and socks and the equally unhurried rolling up of his trouser legs before he waded into the burn which fronts the green.

The high drama at the end of a week of unrelenting attrition and Macbeth-like gloom and doom from many of the much-vaunted "world's best," was rapidly turned into French farce. Jacques Tati's "Monsieur Hulot" would have approved. So would Ben Turpin and Charlie Chaplin, come to think of it.

All week what Carnoustie audiences saw, either in the flesh or worldwide through television, was barely golf as we have come to know it. No succession of birdies and eagles. No barrage of sub-par scoring. Instead, what we saw was golf in the raw, an elemental struggle between man and nature as it was around one hundred years ago when many of Carnoustie's golfing sons headed west for the New World.

Sevens were fairly commonplace, 6s abounded, and there were so many bogey 5s on the first and second days that the people manning the scoreboard in the vast Media Centre used up more than 700 of the blue (for bogey) 5s—each day. Nairn's Sandra Ross has been on duty at the Press Tent scoreboard for the last 20 years and cannot recall having run out of the bogey figures ever before.

"I couldn't believe it," Sandra would recall after the mayhem which created such havoc among the modern game's perceived hierarchy. "By three o'clock in the afternoon of the first day we had to send out an SOS for more blue 5s. An extra 65 were delivered and we used 40 of those before play ended that night. It was the same on the Friday."

Yet there was not even any real wind. Certainly nothing like the gale which vented its full fury on the Angus course during the Amateur Championship in 1992. That year the Press Tent was not only blown down. It was hurled by the furious blasts into the tennis courts more than 100 yards away. All the contenders for the 1999 Open had to put up with was little more than what the good folks of Carnoustie termed a "fresh breeze." The seagulls were never reduced to walking with their heads down against the wind as they do in a proper Carnoustie "blow," for goodness' sake. The beast's real fangs were in the rough, the roughest and toughest I have seen in 34 Opens.

Muirfield's in 1966 looked worse. It appeared to be higher than the corn in Rodgers and Hammerstein's *Oklahoma* which was, as you know, "as high as an elephant's eye." But it was wispy at the home of the Honourable Company of Edinburgh Golfers.

Van de Velde saved par on the 17th in the third round, before good fortune deserted him.

It did not have the jungle-dense properties of the spinach Carnoustie greenkeeper John Philp had carefully prepared and presented. In some places it could have hidden courting couples.

In fairness, the fairways were immaculate and the greens as svelte as the baize on a billiard table. Trouble was only one player was able to take the rough with the smooth, eventual winner Paul Lawrie. It's rather sad, therefore, that the fine upstanding Aberdonian may have the gloss taken off his undoubted heroics through no fault of his own. Without question Paul played the best golf of the week. Yet he could become the target of irksomely sniping, to say nothing of unfair, barbs that he did not so much win the Open, as Van de Velde lost it.

Golf is about as popular in France as a fox in a hen coop, nudist beaches in Antarctica or mobile telephones on aircraft. There are no more than 300,000 participants of "le golf" in a population approaching 60 million and the last Open champion from La Republique was Arnaud Massy back in 1907. So there's not a lot of golfing tradition in the land of fine wines, les escargots and those classy twins, haute cuisine and haute couture. The last Frenchman to challenge for an Open was Jean Garialde at St Andrews in 1964. He played the last two rounds with eventual champion Tony Lema without ever seriously threatening to win.

Then along came Jean Van de Velde. The 33-year-old from the Basque country of Les Landes in southwest France arrived for the 128th Open with a playing record which justified local bookmakers rating him a 200-to-1 outsider. He was ranked 152nd in the world, lay 40th on the PGA European Tour's Volvo Order of Merit, and had to endure the 36-hole qualifying test at nearby Monifieth. Indeed he was so tired after six straight days of competition (he had finished in a tie for 20th in the Standard Life Loch Lomond tournament the previous Saturday before moving straight to the Monifieth qualifying on the Sunday and Monday) that he took Tuesday off and played only practice round.

Few people gave the engaging Frenchman little more than a passing glance. He was regarded as merely one of the extras in the annual extravaganza with little or no form. In his 11 years on the PGA European Tour he had won only once, the Roma Masters in 1993, when he defeated New Zealand's Greg Turner at the third play-off hole. He had also been capable of qualifying for only four Opens before Carnoustie. He missed the cut at Royal Birkdale in 1991, tied for 33rd behind Greg Norman at Royal St George's in 1993, shared 38th at Turnberry the following year, then missed the cut at Royal Troon in 1997. He was a far-from-distinguished 23 over par for those four appearances. Not the stuff of champions.

A first-round 75 at Carnoustie was due in large measure to a devastating putting touch allied to short game wizardry. He had only 24 putts. His putter was used even more sparingly the next day. He limited himself to 23 in a 68 which perched him atop the leaderboard. Then, as golf's cognoscenti waited for him to crumple under the enormity of what he was doing, he had the temerity to add 70 and take an unlikely five-shot lead into the final day.

He did so with the aid of more phenomenal putting, as 27 of his 70 strokes were with his putter, and one outrageous piece of good fortune. He was granted, wrongly it was later admitted, line-of-sight relief at the 11th. He more than rode his good luck to save par when he was staring at least 6 in the face. He followed a 70-foot birdie putt at the 14th with a remarkable sand-save par at the 17th, and the improbable began to look eminently possible. Safely on the green at the treacherous 18th in two, he drained a 45-foot putt for a birdie 3 and a five-stroke advantage over the field. Would he remain cool in the heat of the final day?

Colin Montgomerie was not too sure, saying, "We all know Jean is a very good player, but what we don't know is how he can cope with the situation. It has nothing to do with technique and it has nothing to do with golf. It's all about what's in his head. He now knows where he is and what's happening to him. He'll learn an awful lot about himself and we'll learn an awful lot about Jean Van de Velde over the next 18 holes."

It could well be that Van de Velde, who now lives with wife Brigitte and family in Geneva, is an aquaphobic. Water, in the form of the Barry Burn, did for him at Carnoustie as did a lake on the last hole of the French Open a few years ago. As a kid, Van de Velde lived close to France's gorgeous beaches in and around beautiful Biarritz. His parents loved the sea and all nautical activities. Young Jean, however, was more attracted by the charms of the Hossegor golf course across the fence from the family's holiday

He holed a 70-foot pitch on the 14th in the third round.

home. Eventually, at the age of six or seven, he prevailed upon his parents to introduce him to the game. He was soon addicted.

He has come a long way since those sunny days in short trousers at Hossegor. All the way to leading the Open by five strokes with one round to play. Little could he have expected to live a nightmare as he dropped off to sleep in his Carnoustie hotel that Saturday night on the cushion of his five-stroke advantage.

When it was all over and Paul Lawrie had been crowned, the pragmatist in Van de Velde insisted he had enjoyed himself, that very few people ever had the chance to lead the Open, fewer still to lead by five with 18 holes to play and by three with one to play. His good humour held up better than his golf game and he assured all within earshot that "Next time I lay up with a wedge, OK?"

Sadly, there may not be a next time. Van de Velde proved in the previous 71 holes that he is a player of considerable talent and skill, but what he inflicted upon himself at the 72nd hole will haunt him. His 7 instantly became part of golfing folklore.

For many years to come hackers galore will stand on Carnoustie's 18th tee saying to themselves, "Let's see if I can beat a 7..."

What's the French for triple bogey again? Ah, oui. A Van de Velde!

Paul Lawrie (290) took the lead on this 15-foot putt for birdie on the third hole of the play-off.

GREAT SCOT, WHAT A FINISH

BY ANDY FARRELL

No one before in the history of the Open, covering 127 previous championships, had come from more than five strokes behind to win. Three champions had overcome a five-stroke deficit to hold the silver claret jug. They were Jim Barnes at Prestwick in 1925, Tommy Armour in the first Carnoustie Open in 1931, and Justin Leonard at Royal Troon in 1997. As fate would have it, entering the final round of the 128th Open, Leonard shared second place with Craig Parry, five strokes behind Jean Van de Velde.

Leonard almost repeated the trick the American had performed at Troon and twice elsewhere, including the 1998 Players Championship. Van de Velde should have become the first Frenchman to win the Open since Arnaud Massy at Hoylake in 1907. None of this came to pass. It was all far more extraordinary than that.

Paul Lawrie started the final round at Carnoustie 10 strokes behind Van de Velde. Even when the Scot had finished with a closing 67 and a 290 total, six over par, he thought he had no hope. When Van de Velde teed off at the 72nd hole with a three-stroke lead, he should have had no hope. But the Frenchman took 7 at the last for 77—the how and why still incomprehensible all this time later—and there was a three-way, four-hole play-off involving Van de Velde, Lawrie and Leonard, who had 72.

It felt as if this Open would never put up the "Closed" sign. On it went, the identity of the name to be engraved on the claret jug and the door to the sixth suite in the new Carnoustie Golf Hotel next to those named after Armour, Henry Cotton, Ben Hogan, Gary Player and Tom Watson—all the Carnoustie winners—still unknown. Until, that was, the local boy suddenly birdied the last two holes.

With the approach to the last, a majestic four iron to four feet, the gallery knew, too, they could acclaim one of their own. Then, in the rain and the gloaming, Sir Michael Bonallack, for the last time as Secretary of the Royal and Ancient, was proclaiming Lawrie as the "champion golfer of the year" and the 30-year-old from Aberdeen held the trophy aloft.

Jack Burke Jnr had held the previous record for the biggest comeback in a major championship when he made up a deficit of eight strokes on Ken Venturi to win the 1956 US Masters. Ranked 159th in the world, Lawrie was only the second player from outside the world's top 100—after John Daly twice—to win a major since the rankings were introduced in 1986. Lawrie had come through the qualifying at Downfield, and he became the first qualifier to win the Open since exemptions for the leading players were introduced in 1963.

But all that paled into insignificance beside the fact that Lawrie was the first Scot to win the Open since Sandy Lyle at Sandwich in 1985 and the first Scottish-born player to win in Scotland since Armour here at Carnoustie 68 years before. Even though the "Silver Scot" was born in Edinburgh, he was a naturalised American at the time of his victory. The last home-based Scot to win the Open in Scotland had been Willie Auchterlonie in the last century, at Prestwick in 1893.

"It is a huge thing to win the Open, no matter where it is," Lawrie said, "but obviously here it is extra special, being so close to home. Every kid dreams of winning the Open. There's probably no golfer who doesn't dream of winning the Open."

The sheer unexpectedness of the whole day's proceedings was breathless. You could not say quite the same about the conditions for the final day, but by comparison with the previous days, this was a calm day. Surely, someone would make a move. If it was to be a Scot, Andrew Coltart started the day at seven over par but, playing alongside Tiger Woods, closed with 77. Colin Montgomerie never got going and his

Justin Leonard (290) felt he lost the Open twice in the same day, hitting shots into the Barry Burn.

Craig Parry (291) led before taking 7 at the 12th.

Lawrie's 67 matched the best for the week.

74 left him at 12 over par.

Instead the attention early on had to be turned to Lawrie. His 67 equalled Craig Parry's effort from the previous day as the low round of the week and, despite the improved conditions, was two strokes better than anyone else could manage in the final round.

His start was steady, a shot picked up at the third given away, however, at the fifth. But he holed from 35 feet at the sixth and 25 feet at the eighth to be out in 34. A four iron to three feet at the 12th was not the last brilliant shot he would hit with that club. Now he was seven over par for the championship and moving up the leaderboard.

A shot went at the short 13th, but he got back to seven over by getting up and down from beside the 14th green for a birdie. Then he got to six over par with a 25-footer at the 17th, and he made sure he stayed there at the last. His approach with a five iron from a clumpy lie in the rough skirted over the Barry Burn and rolled into a greenside bunker on the left, but a fine recovery ensured his par.

It was a fine effort, perhaps better even than his last-round 65 to finish sixth in the 1993 Open at Royal St George's. No one then, with the leaders still 90 minutes from finishing, knew quite how much

better. "The way the course is set up, I would have to say that's my best round of golf ever," Lawrie said. "To shoot four under around here, even with no wind, is lovely."

Lawrie was in relaxed mood as he discussed the top-four finish he would almost certainly achieve to book a debut trip to the US Masters, how gaining a place on the European Ryder Cup team might be a possibility, and how pleasing it was to have played four rounds at Carnoustie and not had a double bogey or worse. "That's a big achievement for me because every hole is a potential double bogey, every single one," he said.

He revealed his parents, James, a taxi-driver who would chauffeur him to junior events, and Margaret and his brother, Stephen, were on holiday in Majorca. His wife Marian, who had caddied for him when he first set out on the PGA European Tour, was at home with their sons, Craig, four, and seven-month-old Michael. A week ago, he was not even in the championship.

He played the second nine of the second round at Downfield in four under par just to qualify. "I was desperate to make it," he said. "I was looking forward to coming to Carnoustie. I've won around this course before in the Daily Express Pro-Am in 1991."

Angel Cabrera (291) had 70 to share fourth place.

Greg Norman (293) finished in sixth place alone.

And then someone informed him that four over was now leading on the course.

"Does it really?" Lawrie said. "Where are my sticks? This interview is over. No, I still can't see six over winning. I'll probably be second, third or fourth but you never know, six over could play-off."

Lawrie chatted away some more before concluding the interview. Few others were making a move. Woods still could not make a birdie and abandoned his "safety first" approach from the tee. Pulling out the driver did not help, however, and instead of getting under par for the day, he drove into a bad spot on the 12th, hit his second into an even worse place in a bush by the green, and took his second double bogey of the week. He came home with 74 and finished tied with Davis Love III and David Frost at 294, 10 over par.

Greg Norman managed 72 to finish at 293, and Angel Cabrera rallied after a poor third day with 70 to get into the clubhouse at 291, tied for fourth with Parry, who had 73. Rather than Leonard, of the pair tied for second overnight, it was Parry who made the first move.

Bogeys from Van de Velde at the second and third,

and a birdie by Parry at the latter, put the Australian only two behind. They were tied after a two-shot swing at the short eighth, the Frenchman three-putting from the front edge of the green, Parry holing from 10 feet. Van de Velde then birdied the ninth and Parry, the 10th, but a bogey from Van de Velde at the next put the little Aussie into the lead. He did not hold it for long.

Parry drove into the rough on the 12th, took three to get out of it and three to get down from the back of the green. He took a triple-bogey 7 and the Antipodean challenge was over. He bogeyed the next and took a double bogey at the 17th, eventually tying Cabrera at seven over par.

Despite a second successive bogey at the 12th, Van de Velde was now back in the lead. His nearest rival was Leonard, and the American was looking his solid, reliable self. With the name "Hogan" on his cap, was destiny going to take hold 46 years on from the triumph of the "Wee Ice Mon"?

Destiny, as it turned out, was up to no good elsewhere.

Leonard had one birdie and one bogey for the day playing the 14th. A birdie there brought him into a tie for the lead, but he immediately dropped a shot at the next while Van de Velde, in the group behind, birdied the 14th. Leonard came to the 18th tee two behind. He reached for his three wood, determined to put the ball on the fairway, but saw it leak into the left rough.

Still, it was a good lie. He had 229 yards to the green, 216 to clear the Barry Burn. "I knew Jean was on the green at 17," Leonard said. "I felt I needed to make birdie. It didn't come out the way I hoped, and ended up trickling into the burn."

Leonard took his drop and got up and down for a bogey 5. "At that point, I really didn't think it meant a lot," he said. "I thought I had lost." In the scorer's hut, he signed for 72 that left him on 290, the same six-over total as Lawrie. By now, the Scot had been persuaded out onto the putting green by his coach, Adam Hunter, a former PGA European Tour player.

"Adam did a great job of keeping me focused," Lawrie said. "He was the one who believed six over would win, or at worst get into a play-off."

The first Leonard or Lawrie knew that they might be required again was when they caught sight, from their separate locations, of Van de Velde chipping into the burn at 18. Leonard hurried from the recorder's to the practice range.

Apart from the first day, Van de Velde had played the last four holes—as hard a finishing stretch as you would not want to face trying to win your first major championship—in fine fashion. Again, he parred 15, 16 and 17 and moved three ahead with Leonard's bogey at the last.

"You want to know about the 18th?" Van de Velde said. "I stood there and there is no easy tee shot, I think. Even being three ahead, what do you do? Do you hit a five iron down the left, or do you hit something down the right, or do you try to go as far up as you can? I took that option. I didn't hit a good shot."

The Barry Burn, as well as cutting across in front of the green at the last, horseshoes around the start of the fairway. Van de Velde hit a wild push, but his ball finished to the right of the burn on a little peninsula.

Jim Furyk (295) advanced with his 70.

Retief Goosen (295) secured a top-10 position.

David Frost (294) finished poorly with 74.

Davis Love III (294) rose with 69 to tie for seventh.

"I was lucky to miss the creek," he admitted.

But what to do next? His caddie, Christophe Angiolini, spotted at once he had a "perfect lie. So try for the green." While all around were urging, or later claimed they were urging, the Frenchman to lay up onto the fairway, Van de Velde considered the going-for-the-green option.

"I could not have placed the ball any better and the only thing I had was 189 yards to carry the burn, which wasn't very demanding. The only thing you didn't want to do was hit it left into the out of bounds. So the option was to hit a wedge down the left and pitch on and two-putt or three-putt or whatever, or to try to move forward. The ball was lying so good and I took my two iron and thought, 'You're going to hit it down there. Either you're on the green or just on the right in the bunker or the semi.'"

Again, however, Van de Velde hit a poor shot, pushing the ball to the right. On the plus side, he did clear the burn by some distance. Unfortunately, the ball was heading into the grandstand. Even then, had the ball finished in the stand, he would have got a free drop in the drop zone and would have made no worse than 5. "It was not something absolutely mad

I was trying to do, it just came out to be a nightmare," he lamented.

What happened was a freak bounce. The ball hit the railing of the stand and rebounded backwards towards the burn, bounced off the top of the stone wall of the burn and finished in a horrid tangle of hay. "I would have been better off in the burn, because then I would have had somewhere to drop," he said. "But no, it came back and I had a dramatic lie. I couldn't go backwards, I don't think I could have gone anywhere."

Van de Velde felt this was the shot he would like to take over again, chipping back to the fairway. Instead, he took aim at the green which meant trying to cross the water. He failed to make the carry.

At this point, drama seemed to turn into farce. Van de Velde went to have a look at his ball in the burn, then started to take his shoes and socks off, and clambered down into the water. He couldn't possibly be thinking of playing it, could he?

"When I looked at the ball from short of the green, it looked as if the ball was three-quarters outside the water. As I started to climb down, I could see the ball sinking. It was two or three inches underneath the

Tiger Woods (294) slashed out of the rough to score a par 4 on the fourth hole, one of 11 pars to start the fourth day.

Jean Van de Velde (290) led by three strokes playing the 18th, then took 7 including hitting his third shot into the burn.

Playing along with Van de Velde, Parry holed his bunker shot at the 18th to take a share of fourth place.

water, so there was no hope. It was telling me, 'Hey, you, silly man. Not for you.'"

As Van de Velde put his socks and shoes on, Parry, his playing companion, came across and lightened the moment by suggesting that the tide was going out and he should wait a few minutes. But Van de Velde took his drop and had another bad lie but this time got his pitch over the water and into the right-hand greenside bunker. Parry was in the same bunker and, just when things could not get any more bizarre, the Australian holed from the sand for a birdie.

Van de Velde needed to do the same for 6 and victory. He came out to six feet and holed the putt to get into the play-off.

Outwardly, Van de Velde handled his humiliation with great dignity. In the scorer's hut, he broke down in tears for two minutes. Then he went to his room in the hotel for five minutes to be with his wife, Brigitte. As the traumas for her husband mounted on the 18th, Brigitte was seen on television laughing in disbelief. "Usually, he makes more stupid mistakes on the golf course," she said. "This was the only mistake he made all week."

With the closing 77, Van de Velde was the third player to finish on a total of 290. That meant the winner's score would be the highest for 53 years, but it was only one stroke more than the 289 at which Ian Woosnam won the Scottish Open at Carnoustie in 1996, when the par of the course was 72 instead of 71.

So, for the second year running, a four-hole play-off was required, and when the players assembled on the 15th tee, Van de Velde told his opponents, "I thought it would be better if we kept the entertainment going, and that is why I have invited you to play a few more holes."

Each of the players hit terrible drives. None of them were in sight of the fairway, but while Leonard and Lawrie managed to scramble for 5s, Van de Velde, not surprisingly perhaps, had been so wild he ended up in a bush, had to take an unplayable and ended up with 6.

All three bogeyed the 16th. Was this Open ever going to be won?

Although Van de Velde birdied the 17th, it was Lawrie who provided the answer. With a four iron to 15 feet, he set up a birdie chance that he took to give himself a one-stroke lead over Leonard, who made 4.

The American was the player most expected to triumph from the unlikely threesome, but also with the most to lose. Having taken driver off the 18th tee this time around, amazingly, he put his second into the Barry Burn again. "I had an uphill lie, got a little behind the ball and hit it a hair fat," he said.

Now Lawrie was in command and set another four iron soaring towards the green, giving himself an-

After a poor drive, Leonard had to scramble to make bogey 5 on the first hole of the play-off.

Van de Velde birdied the third play-off hole.

other close birdie chance from three feet. "I was shaking so much, but you don't want to miss a putt to win the Open," Lawrie said. "To birdie the last two holes to win is obviously a fairy story."

Lawrie had a four-hole total of 15, level par, while Leonard and Van de Velde both finished with bogeys and totals of 18.

Leonard felt a double pang of disappointment. "Basically, I lost the Open twice in one day, which is maybe twice as hard to take," he said. "But as bad as I feel, Jean must feel worse. If there is something he can learn from that, it's that he got himself into position to win the tournament."

"You know," Van de Velde said, "I made plenty of friends because a Scottish man won. Maybe I was not humble enough. I didn't need to go for glory. Maybe I should have laid up. But there's worse things in life. I read the newspaper like you this morning, and some terrible things are happening to other people. It is a golf tournament, a game and I gave it my best shot. Next time I hit a wedge, okay, you all forgive me? You say I'm a coward, whatever. Next time I hit a wedge."

Holding the silver trophy, with a cheque for £350,000 and knowing his life was going to change, Lawrie acknowledged the Frenchman's part in his triumph. "Jean should have won. He had it in his pocket, no doubt about that," Lawrie said. "All he

With a four iron to three feet at the last, Lawrie won the Open play-off by three strokes, finishing with two birdies.

had to do was chip it down the fairway and make 5. I'd have chipped it down the fairway. No disrespect, but I'm glad he did what he did.

"On the 15th tee of the play-off, I didn't feel good but the other two seemed as nervous as I was, Justin probably more because he was the one who was expected to win. But when I birdied the 17th, that was the moment I thought I could win. I knew I couldn't see myself bogeying the last. I had practised too hard for that moment.

"I can't explain it, but I had a feeling at the start of the week that someone could come through who wasn't supposed to. With the knee-high rough and some of the big names complaining about it, which they are entitled to do, I felt if I kept quiet and did my own thing, I could come through."

It was an extraordinary win on an extraordinary day to climax an extraordinary Open. "There was triumph, tragedy, romance, farce, pathos and controversy," summarised Hugh Campbell, Chairman of the Championship Committee. "These things follow the Open round."

This was Sir Michael Bonallack's 16th and last Open as Secretary of the R and A. He was not allowed to walk off into the setting sun, since for the first time since he started announcing the winner, it rained on the prize-giving. At least the Open lived up to its ability to surprise right to the end. "I have never seen anything like that in an Open," said Sir Michael. "Mind you, I have never seen anything like it in the monthly medal back home, either."

An extraordinary day finally ended.

Spectators filling the grandstands flanking the last hole and along the new hotel behind the green were witnesses to one of

the most remarkable finishes in the history of the Open Championship.

FOURTH ROUND RESULTS

HOLE	1	2	3	4	5	6	7	8	9	10	11	12	13	14	15	16	17	18	TOTAL
PAR	4	4	4	4	4	5	4	3	4	4	4	4	3	5	4	3	4	4	TOTAL
Paul Lawrie	4	4	3	4	5	4	4	2	4	4	4	3	4	4	4	3	3	4	67-290
															5	4	3	3	15
Justin Leonard	4	4	4	4	4	4	4	3	4	5	4	4	3	4	5	3	4	5	72-290
															5	4	4	5	18
Jean Van de Velde	4	5	5	4	4	5	4	4	3	4	5	5	3	4	4	3	4	7	77-290
															6	4	3	5	18
Angel Cabrera	4	4	3	4	4	5	4	4	4	4	3	4	4	5	4	3	4	4	70-291
Craig Parry	4	4	3	4	4	5	4	2	4	3	4	7	4	5	4	3	6	3	73-291
Greg Norman	4	4	4	5	5	5	4	3	4	4	4	4	3	4	4	3	4	5	72-293
Davis Love III	4	3	4	3	4	5	3	4	5	5	3	5	2	4	4	4	4	3	69-294
Tiger Woods	4	4	4	4	4	5	4	3	4	4	4	6	3	4	5	3	4	5	74-294
David Frost	5	6	3	5	6	4	3	4	4	4	4	5	2	4	4	4	4	4	74-294
Jim Furyk	4	3	3	4	4	5	4	3	3	5	4	3	3	4	6	4	4	4	70-295
Scott Dunlap	3	3	4	4	5	6	4	4	4	4	4	4	2	4	4	2	4	5	70-295
Retief Goosen	4	4	5	4	4	5	3	4	3	5	4	4	3	4	4	3	4	4	71-295
Jesper Parnevik	5	4	3	4	5	4	4	4	4	4	3	6	2	4	4	3	3	6	72-295
Hal Sutton	3	4	4	4	4	5	5	4	3	3	3	4	4	5	4	3	4	6	72-295
Scott Verplank	4	3	4	5	4	4	4	3	4	4	4	4	2	4	4	3	4	5	69-296
Tsuyoshi Yoneyama	4	3	4	4	5	4	4	4	5	5	4	4	3	4	5	3	4	3	72-296
Colin Montgomerie	5	4	4	4	4	5	4	3	3	7	4	4	3	5	4	3	4	4	74-296

HOLE SUMMARY

HOLE	PAR	EAGLES	BIRDIES	PARS	BOGEYS	HIGHER	RANK	AVERAGE
1	4	0	12	49	11	1	14	4.01
2	4	0	11	45	13	4	10	4.15
3	4	0	16	47	9	1	17	3.95
4	4	0	7	50	16	0	12	4.12
5	4	0	3	46	21	3	6	4.33
6	5	0	15	33	21	4	9	5.19
7	4	0	8	50	13	2	12	4.12
8	3	0	6	44	22	1	7	3.25
9	4	0	6	38	25	4	5	4.37
OUT	36	0	84	402	151	20		37.49
10	4	0	3	42	20	8	3	4.48
11	4	0	13	49	10	1	15	4.00
12	4	0	3	34	26	10	1	4.63
13	3	0	14	50	7	2	16	2.96
14	5	0	36	30	6	1	18	4.63
15	4	0	0	41	27	5	2	4.51
16	3	0	8	47	18	0	11	3.14
17	4	0	9	44	16	4	8	4.22
18	4	0	5	37	23	8	3	4.48
IN	35	0	91	374	153	39		37.04
TOTAL	71	0	175	776	304	59		74.53

Players Below Par	8
Players At Par	1
Players Above Par	64

LOW SCORES

Low First Nine	Peter O'Malley	33
	Jim Furyk	33
Low Second Nine	Thomas Bjorn	32
Low Round	Paul Lawrie	67

WEATHER

Temperature: low 11°C, high 20°C.
Light southeast breeze.

CHAMPIONSHIP HOLE SUMMARY

HOLE	PAR	YARDS	EAGLES	BIRDIES	PARS	BOGEYS	HIGHER	RANK	AVERAGE
1	4	407	0	37	277	122	20	14	4.28
2	4	462	0	37	270	121	28	13	4.31
3	4	342	1	61	313	73	8	16	4.06
4	4	412	0	33	259	140	24	10	4.35
5	4	411	0	35	270	127	24	12	4.31
6	5	578	0	34	219	157	46	4	5.49
7	4	412	1	30	228	152	45	5	4.47
8	3	183	0	44	264	132	16	15	3.27
9	4	474	0	23	207	178	48	1	4.57
OUT	36	3681	2	334	2307	1202	259		39.11
10	4	466	1	37	241	143	34	8	4.39
11	4	383	0	31	270	132	23	11	4.33
12	4	479	0	13	227	167	49	2	4.57
13	3	169	0	66	317	69	4	17	3.02
14	5	515	11	234	173	33	5	18	4.54
15	4	472	0	23	233	172	28	6	4.46
16	3	250	0	21	252	169	14	9	3.39
17	4	459	0	24	217	162	53	2	4.57
18	4	487	0	35	235	140	46	7	4.45
IN	35	3680	12	484	2165	1187	256		37.70
TOTAL	71	7361	14	818	4472	2389	515		76.82

	FIRST ROUND	SECOND ROUND	THIRD ROUND	FOURTH ROUND	TOTAL
Players Below Par	0	7	3	8	18
Players At Par	1	6	2	1	10
Players Above Par	155	141	68	64	428

RELATIVE DIFFICULTY OF HOLES

HOLE	PAR	YARDS	FIRST ROUND	SECOND ROUND	THIRD ROUND	FOURTH ROUND	OVERALL RANK
1	4	407	14	12	12	14	14
2	4	462	15	8	11	10	13
3	4	342	16	17	17	17	16
4	4	412	13	11	3	12	10
5	4	411	11	15	14	6	12
6	5	578	3	3	7	9	4
7	4	412	5	5	2	12	5
8	3	183	12	13	15	7	15
9	4	474	1	4	4	5	1
10	4	466	7	14	7	3	8
11	4	383	10	10	13	15	11
12	4	479	4	2	5	1	2
13	3	169	17	16	16	16	17
14	5	515	18	18	18	18	18
15	4	472	8	8	6	2	6
16	3	250	9	6	9	11	9
17	4	459	2	1	1	8	2
18	4	487	6	6	9	3	7

Applause from his fellow Scots greeted Paul Lawrie as he reached the last green, having a three-foot putt for birdie.

COMMENTARY

IT JUST HAS TO BE TRUE

BY JOHN HOPKINS

As a boy growing up in Aberdeen, the granite city in the north of Scotland, Paul Lawrie became accustomed to the highs and lows of his hometown's football team. Little did Lawrie think that one day his deeds on a golf course would become as much a part of folklore in the city of his birth as Aberdeen winning the 1983 Cup Winners' Cup.

But that is the magic of sport. Every so often it throws up a story so impossible it just has to be true. On Monday 12 July, Lawrie awoke with one target in mind—to qualify for the Open. On Monday 19 July, Lawrie awoke with a priceless asset in his eyeline—the Open trophy. It sat on the floor of his sitting room where it had been ever since he got home just before midnight the previous night, the most remarkable day of his life. The day that had begun with Lawrie leaving his house soon after breakfast when he was 10 strokes behind Jean Van de Velde had ended with him returning as the Open champion.

Lawrie is only the seventh British player since the war to claim one of the game's most prized trophies, following Fred Daly in 1947, Henry Cotton in 1948, Max Faulkner in 1951, Tony Jacklin in 1969, Sandy Lyle in 1985 and Nick Faldo in 1987, 1990 and 1992.

It hardly matters that he is the most unlikely winner. Not even his parents believed he was going to feature in the Open, because that week they were on holiday with Stephen, their other son, and all three watched the excitement unfold in a bar in Majorca.

Lawrie was born on New Year's Day 1969 and began playing golf as soon as he was tall enough to swing a club. He played off a handicap of 4 and had no amateur pedigree when he turned professional, aged 17, and started working as an assistant professional with the late Doug Smart at Banchory Golf Club near Aberdeen.

About this time Smart was giving a journalist a lesson on the practice ground and there was Lawrie, practising. "Believe me," Smart said. "That boy is made of the right stuff. He has a great future. I have had boys who turn pro with me with far better amateur records but there is something different about him. I have a feeling about him." Sadly, Smart was not able to see the truth of those words. In 1993 he took his own life after suffering deep depression after giving up his post at Banchory and then being diagnosed as having lip cancer.

Victory in a major championship will not have changed Lawrie's life; it will have transformed it. From being a struggling journeyman pro with only two victories in Europe to his credit, the man who was close to giving up tournament golf in 1995 because of his poor form turned himself into a millionaire and won himself the right to enter competitions such as the World Golf Championship events at which the prize money is $5 million. He won himself a place on the Ryder Cup team as well as guaranteeing himself a place in the US Masters, US Open, Open and USPGA Championship for the next five years.

Lawrie knew he could win at Carnoustie—or at least he thought he could—because he had won a pro-am there in 1991 and played between 25 and 30 rounds over the famous Angus course, an hour's drive south of his home. That, though, was hardly the Carnoustie over which the 128th Open was played, the Carnoustie with waisted fairways and longer-than-usual rough. Early in the week of the Open he had said to his brother-in-law that he felt someone unexpected would win the Open. "The fairways are narrow, the rough is up and many of the best-known players were not happy about the set-up. I just felt that if I kept quiet and did my own thing I could come through."

When he did so, it completed one of the most extraordinary sequences of play there can ever have been. Lawrie launched himself on a career as a touring professional in 1992 and until the Open it had been notable for being ordinary. But what was about to happen now was straight out of the pages of old-fashioned magazines.

It went like this: The son of a taxi-driver in Aberdeen, ranked 159th in the world, plays the round of his life, 67, over one of the hardest golf courses in the world and as a result comes from 10 strokes behind to claim the oldest major championship in golf. In doing so he is helped by a Frenchman whose attachment is to the Disneyland complex near Paris who had appeared certain to win only to appear to lose his faculties on the last hole of regulation play. Also involved in the play-off is a 27-year-old American who won the Open in 1997 and has won more tournaments than his two rivals combined. Initially all three men play like weekend amateurs before Lawrie transforms himself with two brilliant iron shots that set up the most improbable victory this century by three strokes.

Lawrie is at a loss to explain how, after years of being an ordinary professional, he was suddenly transformed into one of the best in the world; how, after missing seven out of 16 tournament cuts this year, he first qualified and then became one of the very few golfers to go through all the qualifying events and win the Open. "Why does anyone peak when they do?" he asked. "I don't know why it took Mark O'Meara until he was 40 to win a major championship."

But neither does Lawrie know whether his golf can remain at the standard it reached in Carnoustie rather than return to what it had been before, which, frankly, had not been very good. He had never been higher than 21st in the Order of Merit and his victory in the Open was £90,000 more than his earnings in 1996, his most lucrative season.

As the media focus magnified on Lawrie, his attitude to the pressure was encouraging. He is certainly fully aware of his new position. "No matter what I do now, people are going to say, 'What did Lawrie do? Oh, he's three over, he's lost it.' I don't have a problem with that. The Ryder Cup, the major championships, these are things that you dream about playing in. Obviously when I get to the Ryder Cup it is going to be quite tough for me, but I've always felt that I was good enough to play in it and all of a sudden the opportunity has arisen."

The world of golf is not so large that coincidences cannot occur and there is one that links Nick Faldo with Paul Lawrie. Faldo was 30 when he won his first major championship, the same age as Lawrie when he won his. Faldo had been taught by David Leadbetter and so, briefly, was Lawrie who met Leadbetter at a London airport in 1995, a time when the Scot was frustrated with his game and desperate for guidance. While David Whelan, an assistant of Leadbetter, supervised Lawrie's development on a regular basis, Leadbetter studied Lawrie's progress on video each winter when Lawrie and a group of fellow Scots visited Leadbetter's home base, Lake Nona, in Orlando, Florida.

Thus it was that Leadbetter was able to appear less surprised than most by Lawrie's success. "I predicted a few years ago that Paul had what it takes to be a real danger in the Open," Leadbetter said. "There was something about him that made him stand out. It is an indefinable quality that sets him apart from the rest. He has the calmness and utter confidence that a champion needs. More than anything, he has that bit of courage for the big time. When his chance came, it did not surprise me that he took it.

"Paul will go from strength to strength. He has a lot to learn but he is very talented and prepared to work. He will have to learn to fly the ball higher to suit the conditions in the US," Leadbetter said. "That was something we were working on with him. He will also have to pace himself, not rush to cash in on his success and become burned out. He can play with the big boys now. He showed it in overcoming Justin Leonard in the play-off. There is no greater pressure than that."

"I predicted a few years ago," said David Leadbetter, "that Paul had what it takes to be a real danger in the Open."

Tom Lehman (1996)

Nick Faldo (1987, 1990, 1992)

Greg Norman (1986, 1993)

Mark O'Meara (1998)

Nick Price (1994)

Justin Leonard (1997)

OPEN CHAMPIONSHIP

YEAR	CHAMPION	SCORE	MARGIN	RUNNERS-UP	VENUE
1860	Willie Park	174	2	Tom Morris Snr	Prestwick
1861	Tom Morris Snr	163	4	Willie Park	Prestwick
1862	Tom Morris Snr	163	13	Willie Park	Prestwick
1863	Willie Park	168	2	Tom Morris Snr	Prestwick
1864	Tom Morris Snr	167	2	Andrew Strath	Prestwick
1865	Andrew Strath	162	2	Willie Park	Prestwick
1866	Willie Park	169	2	David Park	Prestwick
1867	Tom Morris Snr	170	2	Willie Park	Prestwick
1868	Tom Morris Jnr	157	2	Robert Andrew	Prestwick
1869	Tom Morris Jnr	154	3	Tom Morris Snr	Prestwick
1870	Tom Morris Jnr	149	12	Bob Kirk, David Strath	Prestwick
1871	*No Competition*				
1872	Tom Morris Jnr	166	3	David Strath	Prestwick
1873	Tom Kidd	179	1	Jamie Anderson	St Andrews
1874	Mungo Park	159	2	Tom Morris Jnr	Musselburgh
1875	Willie Park	166	2	Bob Martin	Prestwick
1876	Bob Martin	176	—	David Strath	St Andrews
				(Martin was awarded the title when Strath refused to play-off)	
1877	Jamie Anderson	160	2	Bob Pringle	Musselburgh
1878	Jamie Anderson	157	2	Bob Kirk	Prestwick
1879	Jamie Anderson	169	3	James Allan, Andrew Kirkaldy	St Andrews
1880	Bob Ferguson	162	5	Peter Paxton	Musselburgh
1881	Bob Ferguson	170	3	Jamie Anderson	Prestwick
1882	Bob Ferguson	171	3	Willie Fernie	St Andrews
1883	Willie Fernie	159	Play-off	Bob Ferguson	Musselburgh
				(Fernie won play-off 158 to 159)	
1884	Jack Simpson	160	4	David Rollan, Willie Fernie	Prestwick
1885	Bob Martin	171	1	Archie Simpson	St Andrews
1886	David Brown	157	2	Willie Campbell	Musselburgh
1887	Willie Park Jnr	161	1	Bob Martin	Prestwick
1888	Jack Burns	171	1	David Anderson Jnr, Ben Sayers	St Andrews
1889	Willie Park Jnr	155	Play-off	Andrew Kirkaldy	Musselburgh
				(Park won play-off 158 to 163)	
1890	*John Ball	164	3	Willie Fernie, Archie Simpson	Prestwick
1891	Hugh Kirkaldy	166	2	Willie Fernie, Andrew Kirkaldy	St Andrews
(From 1892 the competition was extended to 72 holes)					
1892	*Harold Hilton	305	3	*John Ball Jnr, James Kirkaldy, Sandy Herd	Muirfield
1893	Willie Auchterlonie	322	2	*Johnny Laidlay	Prestwick
1894	J.H. Taylor	326	5	Douglas Rolland	Sandwich

YEAR	CHAMPION	SCORE	MARGIN	RUNNERS-UP	VENUE
1895	J.H. Taylor	322	4	Sandy Herd	St Andrews
1896	Harry Vardon	316	Play-off	J.H. Taylor	Muirfield
				(Vardon won play-off 157 to 161)	
1897	*Harold H. Hilton	314	1	James Braid	Hoylake
1898	Harry Vardon	307	1	Willie Park	Prestwick
1899	Harry Vardon	310	5	Jack White	Sandwich
1900	J.H. Taylor	309	8	Harry Vardon	St Andrews
1901	James Braid	309	3	Harry Vardon	Muirfield
1902	Sandy Herd	307	1	Harry Vardon, James Braid	Hoylake
1903	Harry Vardon	300	6	Tom Vardon	Prestwick
1904	Jack White	296	1	James Braid, J.H. Taylor	Sandwich
1905	James Braid	318	5	J.H. Taylor, R. Jones	St Andrews
1906	James Braid	300	4	J.H. Taylor	Muirfield
1907	Arnaud Massy	312	2	J.H. Taylor	Hoylake
1908	James Braid	291	8	Tom Ball	Prestwick
1909	J.H. Taylor	295	4	James Braid	Deal
1910	James Braid	299	4	Sandy Herd	St Andrews
1911	Harry Vardon	303	Play-off	Arnaud Massy	Sandwich
				(Play-off; Massy conceded at the 35th hole)	
1912	Ted Ray	295	4	Harry Vardon	Muirfield
1913	J.H. Taylor	304	8	Ted Ray	Hoylake
1914	Harry Vardon	306	3	J.H. Taylor	Prestwick
1915-1919 No Championship					
1920	George Duncan	303	2	Sandy Herd	Deal
1921	Jock Hutchison	296	Play-off	*Roger Wethered	St Andrews
				(Hutchison won play-off 150 to 159)	
1922	Walter Hagen	300	1	George Duncan, Jim Barnes	Sandwich
1923	Arthur G. Havers	295	1	Walter Hagen	Troon
1924	Walter Hagen	301	1	Ernest Whitcombe	Hoylake
1925	Jim Barnes	300	1	Archie Compston, Ted Ray	Prestwick
1926	*Robert T. Jones Jnr	291	2	Al Watrous	Royal Lytham
1927	*Robert T. Jones Jnr	285	6	Aubrey Boomer, Fred Robson	St Andrews
1928	Walter Hagen	292	2	Gene Sarazen	Sandwich
1929	Walter Hagen	292	6	John Farrell	Muirfield
1930	*Robert T. Jones Jnr	291	2	Leo Diegel, Macdonald Smith	Hoylake
1931	Tommy Armour	296	1	Jose Jurado	Carnoustie
1932	Gene Sarazen	283	5	Macdonald Smith	Prince's
1933	Densmore Shute	292	Play-off	Craig Wood	St Andrews
				(Shute won play-off 149 to 154)	
1934	Henry Cotton	283	5	Sid Brews	Sandwich
1935	Alf Perry	283	4	Alf Padgham	Muirfield
1936	Alf Padgham	287	1	Jimmy Adams	Hoylake
1937	Henry Cotton	290	2	Reg Whitcombe	Carnoustie
1938	Reg Whitcombe	295	2	Jimmy Adams	Sandwich
1939	Richard Burton	290	2	Johnny Bulla	St Andrews
1940-1945 No Championship					
1946	Sam Snead	290	4	Bobby Locke, Johnny Bulla	St Andrews
1947	Fred Daly	293	1	Reg Horne, *Frank Stranahan	Hoylake
1948	Henry Cotton	284	5	Fred Daly	Muirfield
1949	Bobby Locke	283	Play-off	Harry Bradshaw	Sandwich
				(Locke won play-off 135 to 147)	
1950	Bobby Locke	279	2	Roberto de Vicenzo	Troon
1951	Max Faulkner	285	2	Tony Cerda	Royal Portrush
1952	Bobby Locke	287	1	Peter Thomson	Royal Lytham
1953	Ben Hogan	282	4	*Frank Stranahan, Dai Rees,	Carnoustie
				Peter Thomson, Tony Cerda	

YEAR	CHAMPION	SCORE	MARGIN	RUNNERS-UP	VENUE
1954	Peter Thomson	283	1	Sid Scott, Dai Rees, Bobby Locke	Royal Birkdale
1955	Peter Thomson	281	2	Johnny Fallon	St Andrews
1956	Peter Thomson	286	3	Flory van Donck	Hoylake
1957	Bobby Locke	279	3	Peter Thomson	St Andrews
1958	Peter Thomson	278	Play-off	David Thomas	Royal Lytham
				(Thomson won play-off 139 to 143)	
1959	Gary Player	284	2	Flory van Donck, Fred Bullock	Muirfield
1960	Kel Nagle	278	1	Arnold Palmer	St Andrews
1961	Arnold Palmer	284	1	Dai Rees	Royal Birkdale
1962	Arnold Palmer	276	6	Kel Nagle	Troon
1963	Bob Charles	277	Play-off	Phil Rodgers	Royal Lytham
				(Charles won play-off 140 to 148)	
1964	Tony Lema	279	5	Jack Nicklaus	St Andrews
1965	Peter Thomson	285	2	Christy O'Connor, Brian Huggett	Royal Birkdale
1966	Jack Nicklaus	282	1	David Thomas, Doug Sanders	Muirfield
1967	Roberto de Vicenzo	278	2	Jack Nicklaus	Hoylake
1968	Gary Player	289	2	Jack Nicklaus, Bob Charles	Carnoustie
1969	Tony Jacklin	280	2	Bob Charles	Royal Lytham
1970	Jack Nicklaus	283	Play-off	Doug Sanders	St Andrews
				(Nicklaus won play-off 72 to 73)	
1971	Lee Trevino	278	1	Lu Liang Huan	Royal Birkdale
1972	Lee Trevino	278	1	Jack Nicklaus	Muirfield
1973	Tom Weiskopf	276	3	Neil Coles, Johnny Miller	Troon
1974	Gary Player	282	4	Peter Oosterhuis	Royal Lytham
1975	Tom Watson	279	Play-off	Jack Newton	Carnoustie
				(Watson won play-off 71 to 72)	
1976	Johnny Miller	279	6	Jack Nicklaus, Severiano Ballesteros	Royal Birkdale
1977	Tom Watson	268	1	Jack Nicklaus	Turnberry
1978	Jack Nicklaus	281	2	Simon Owen, Ben Crenshaw, Raymond Floyd, Tom Kite	St Andrews
1979	Severiano Ballesteros	283	3	Jack Nicklaus, Ben Crenshaw	Royal Lytham
1980	Tom Watson	271	4	Lee Trevino	Muirfield
1981	Bill Rogers	276	4	Bernhard Langer	Sandwich
1982	Tom Watson	284	1	Peter Oosterhuis, Nick Price	Troon
1983	Tom Watson	275	1	Hale Irwin, Andy Bean	Royal Birkdale
1984	Severiano Ballesteros	276	2	Bernhard Langer, Tom Watson	St Andrews
1985	Sandy Lyle	282	1	Payne Stewart	Sandwich
1986	Greg Norman	280	5	Gordon J. Brand	Turnberry
1987	Nick Faldo	279	1	Rodger Davis, Paul Azinger	Muirfield
1988	Severiano Ballesteros	273	2	Nick Price	Royal Lytham
1989	Mark Calcavecchia	275	Play-off	Greg Norman, Wayne Grady	Royal Troon
				(Calcavecchia won four-hole play-off)	
1990	Nick Faldo	270	5	Mark McNulty, Payne Stewart	St Andrews
1991	Ian Baker-Finch	272	2	Mike Harwood	Royal Birkdale
1992	Nick Faldo	272	1	John Cook	Muirfield
1993	Greg Norman	267	2	Nick Faldo	Sandwich
1994	Nick Price	268	1	Jesper Parnevik	Turnberry
1995	John Daly	282	Play-off	Costantino Rocca	St Andrews
				(Daly won four-hole play-off)	
1996	Tom Lehman	271	2	Mark McCumber, Ernie Els	Royal Lytham
1997	Justin Leonard	272	3	Jesper Parnevik, Darren Clarke	Royal Troon
1998	Mark O'Meara	280	Play-off	Brian Watts	Royal Birkdale
				(O'Meara won four-hole play-off)	
1999	Paul Lawrie	290	Play-off	Justin Leonard Jean Van de Velde	Carnoustie
				(Lawrie won four-hole play-off)	

*Denotes amateurs

Bob Charles (1963)

Sandy Lyle (1985)

Tony Jacklin (1969)

Gary Player (1959, 1968, 1974)

Seve Ballesteros (1979, 1984, 1988)

Tom Watson (1975, 1977, 1980, 1982, 1983)

Mark Calcavecchia (1989)

OPEN CHAMPIONSHIP

MOST VICTORIES
6, Harry Vardon, 1896-98-99-1903-11-14
5, James Braid, 1901-05-06-08-10; J.H. Taylor, 1894-95-1900-09-13; Peter Thomson, 1954-55-56-58-65; Tom Watson, 1975-77-80-82-83

MOST TIMES RUNNER-UP OR JOINT RUNNER-UP
7, Jack Nicklaus, 1964-67-68-72-76-77-79
6, J.H. Taylor, 1896-1904-05-06-07-14

OLDEST WINNER
Old Tom Morris, 46 years 99 days, 1867
Roberto de Vicenzo, 44 years 93 days, 1967

YOUNGEST WINNER
Young Tom Morris, 17 years 5 months 8 days, 1868
Willie Auchterlonie, 21 years 24 days, 1893
Severiano Ballesteros, 22 years 3 months 12 days, 1979

YOUNGEST AND OLDEST COMPETITOR
Young Tom Morris, 14 years 4 months 4 days, 1865
Gene Sarazen, 71 years 4 months 13 days, 1973

BIGGEST MARGIN OF VICTORY
13 strokes, Old Tom Morris, 1862
12 strokes, Young Tom Morris, 1870
8 strokes, J.H. Taylor, 1900 and 1913; James Braid, 1908
6 strokes, Bobby Jones, 1927; Walter Hagen, 1929; Arnold Palmer, 1962; Johnny Miller, 1976

LOWEST WINNING AGGREGATES
267 (66, 68, 69, 64), Greg Norman, Royal St George's, 1993
268 (68, 70, 65, 65), Tom Watson, Turnberry, 1977; (69, 66, 67, 66), Nick Price, Turnberry, 1994
270 (67, 65, 67, 71), Nick Faldo, St Andrews, 1990

LOWEST AGGREGATES BY RUNNER-UP
269 (68, 70, 65, 66), Jack Nicklaus, Turnberry, 1977; (69, 63, 70, 67), Nick Faldo, Royal St George's, 1993; (68, 66, 68, 67), Jesper Parnevik, Turnberry, 1994

LOWEST AGGREGATE BY AN AMATEUR
281 (68, 72, 70, 71), Iain Pyman, Royal St George's, 1993; (75, 66, 70, 70), Tiger Woods, Royal Lytham, 1996

LOWEST INDIVIDUAL ROUND
63, Mark Hayes, second round, Turnberry, 1977; Isao Aoki, third round, Muirfield, 1980; Greg Norman, second round, Turnberry, 1986; Paul Broadhurst, third round, St Andrews, 1990; Jodie Mudd, fourth round, Royal Birkdale, 1991; Nick Faldo, second round, and Payne Stewart, fourth round, Royal St George's, 1993

LOWEST INDIVIDUAL ROUND BY AN AMATEUR
66, Frank Stranahan, fourth round, Troon, 1950; Tiger Woods, second round, Royal Lytham, 1996; Justin Rose, second round, Royal Birkdale, 1998

LOWEST FIRST ROUND
64, Craig Stadler, Royal Birkdale, 1983; Christy O'Connor Jr., Royal St George's, 1985; Rodger Davis, Muirfield, 1987; Raymond Floyd and Steve Pate, Muirfield, 1992

LOWEST SECOND ROUND
63, Mark Hayes, Turnberry, 1977; Greg Norman, Turnberry, 1986; Nick Faldo, Royal St George's, 1993

LOWEST THIRD ROUND
63, Isao Aoki, Muirfield, 1980; Paul Broadhurst, St Andrews, 1990

LOWEST FOURTH ROUND
63, Jodie Mudd, Royal Birkdale, 1991; Payne Stewart, Royal St George's, 1993

LOWEST FIRST 36 HOLES
130 (66, 64), Nick Faldo, Muirfield, 1992

LOWEST SECOND 36 HOLES
130 (65, 65), Tom Watson, Turnberry, 1977; (64, 66), Ian Baker-Finch, Royal Birkdale, 1991; (66, 64), Anders Forsbrand, Turnberry, 1994

LOWEST FIRST 54 HOLES
198 (67, 67, 64), Tom Lehman, Royal Lytham, 1996

LOWEST FINAL 54 HOLES
199 (66, 67, 66), Nick Price, Turnberry, 1994

LOWEST 9 HOLES
28, Denis Durnian, first 9, Royal Birkdale, 1983
29, Peter Thomson and Tom Haliburton, first 9, Royal

Lytham, 1958; Tony Jacklin, first 9, St Andrews, 1970; Bill Longmuir, first 9, Royal Lytham, 1979; David J. Russell, first 9, Royal Lytham, 1988; Ian Baker-Finch and Paul Broadhurst, first 9, St Andrews, 1990; Ian Baker-Finch, first 9, Royal Birkdale, 1991; Paul McGinley, first 9, Royal Lytham, 1996

CHAMPIONS IN THREE DECADES
Harry Vardon, 1896, 1903, 1911
J.H. Taylor, 1894, 1900, 1913
Gary Player, 1959, 1968, 1974

BIGGEST SPAN BETWEEN FIRST AND LAST VICTORIES
19 years, J.H. Taylor, 1894-1913
18 years, Harry Vardon, 1896-1914
15 years, Gary Player, 1959-74
14 years, Henry Cotton, 1934-48

SUCCESSIVE VICTORIES
4, Young Tom Morris, 1868-72. No championship in 1871
3, Jamie Anderson, 1877-79; Bob Ferguson, 1880-82, Peter Thomson, 1954-56
2, Old Tom Morris, 1861-62; J.H. Taylor, 1894-95; Harry Vardon, 1898-99; James Braid, 1905-06; Bobby Jones, 1926-27; Walter Hagen, 1928-29; Bobby Locke, 1949-50; Arnold Palmer, 1961-62; Lee Trevino, 1971-72; Tom Watson, 1982-83

VICTORIES BY AMATEURS
3, Bobby Jones, 1926-27-30
2, Harold Hilton, 1892-97
1, John Ball, 1890
Roger Wethered lost a play-off in 1921

HIGHEST NUMBER OF TOP FIVE FINISHES
16, J.H. Taylor, Jack Nicklaus
15, Harry Vardon, James Braid

HIGHEST NUMBER OF ROUNDS UNDER 70
33, Jack Nicklaus, Nick Faldo
27, Tom Watson
23, Greg Norman
21, Lee Trevino
20, Severiano Ballesteros, Nick Price

OUTRIGHT LEADER AFTER EVERY ROUND
Willie Auchterlonie, 1893; J.H. Taylor, 1894 and 1900; James Braid, 1908; Ted Ray, 1912; Bobby Jones, 1927; Gene Sarazen, 1932; Henry Cotton, 1934; Tom Weiskopf, 1973

RECORD LEADS (SINCE 1892)
After 18 holes:
4 strokes, James Braid, 1908; Bobby Jones, 1927; Henry Cotton, 1934; Christy O'Connor Jr., 1985
After 36 holes:
9 strokes, Henry Cotton, 1934
After 54 holes:
10 strokes, Henry Cotton, 1934
7 strokes, Tony Lema, 1964
6 strokes, James Braid, 1908; Tom Lehman, 1996

CHAMPIONS WITH EACH ROUND LOWER THAN PREVIOUS ONE
Jack White, 1904, Sandwich, (80, 75, 72, 69)
James Braid, 1906, Muirfield, (77, 76, 74, 73)
Ben Hogan, 1953, Carnoustie, (73, 71, 70, 68)
Gary Player, 1959, Muirfield, (75, 71, 70, 68)

CHAMPION WITH FOUR ROUNDS THE SAME
Densmore Shute, 1933, St Andrews, (73, 73, 73, 73) (excluding the play-off)

BIGGEST VARIATION BETWEEN ROUNDS OF A CHAMPION
14 strokes, Henry Cotton, 1934, second round 65, fourth round 79
11 strokes, Jack White, 1904, first round 80, fourth round 69; Greg Norman, 1986, first round 74, second round 63, third round 74

BIGGEST VARIATION BETWEEN TWO ROUNDS
18 strokes, A. Tingey Jr., 1923, first round 94, second round 76
17 strokes, Jack Nicklaus, 1981, first round 83, second round 66; Ian Baker-Finch, 1986, first round 86, second round 69

BEST COMEBACK BY CHAMPIONS
After 18 holes:
Harry Vardon, 1896, 11 strokes behind the leader
After 36 holes:
George Duncan, 1920, 13 strokes behind the leader
After 54 holes:
Paul Lawrie, 1999, 10 strokes behind the leader
Of non-champions, Greg Norman, 1989, 7 strokes behind the leader and lost in a play-off

CHAMPIONS WITH FOUR ROUNDS UNDER 70
Greg Norman, 1993, Royal St George's, (66, 68, 69, 64); Nick Price, 1994, Turnberry, (69, 66, 67, 66)
Of non-champions:
Ernie Els, 1993, Royal St George's, (68, 69, 69, 68); Jesper Parnevik, 1994, Turnberry, (68, 66, 68, 67)

BEST FINISHING ROUND BY A CHAMPION
64, Greg Norman, Royal St George's, 1993
65, Tom Watson, Turnberry, 1977; Severiano Ballesteros, Royal Lytham, 1988; Justin Leonard, Royal Troon, 1997
66, Johnny Miller, Royal Birkdale, 1976; Ian Baker-Finch, Royal Birkdale, 1991; Nick Price, Turnberry, 1994

WORST FINISHING ROUND BY A CHAMPION SINCE 1920
79, Henry Cotton, Sandwich, 1934
78, Reg Whitcombe, Sandwich, 1938
77, Walter Hagen, Hoylake, 1924

WORST OPENING ROUND BY A CHAMPION SINCE 1919
80, George Duncan, Deal, 1920 (he also had a second round of 80)
77, Walter Hagen, Hoylake, 1924

BEST OPENING ROUND BY A CHAMPION
66, Peter Thomson, Royal Lytham, 1958; Nick Faldo, Muirfield, 1992; Greg Norman, Royal St George's, 1993

BIGGEST RECOVERY IN 18 HOLES BY A CHAMPION
George Duncan, Deal, 1920, was 13 strokes behind the leader, Abe Mitchell, after 36 holes and level after 54

MOST APPEARANCES ON FINAL DAY (SINCE 1892)
32, Jack Nicklaus
30, J.H. Taylor
27, Harry Vardon, James Braid
26, Peter Thomson, Gary Player
23, Dai Rees
22, Henry Cotton

CHAMPIONSHIP WITH HIGHEST NUMBER OF ROUNDS UNDER 70
148, Turnberry, 1994

CHAMPIONSHIP SINCE 1946 WITH THE FEWEST ROUNDS UNDER 70
St Andrews, 1946; Hoylake, 1947; Portrush, 1951; Hoylake, 1956; Carnoustie, 1968. All had only two rounds under 70

LONGEST COURSE
Carnoustie, 1999, 7361 yd

COURSES MOST OFTEN USED
St Andrews, 25; Prestwick, 24; Muirfield, 14; Sandwich, 12; Hoylake, 10; Royal Lytham, 9; Royal Birkdale, 8; Royal Troon, 7; Musselburgh and Carnoustie, 6; Turnberry, 3; Deal, 2; Royal Portrush and Prince's, 1

PRIZE MONEY

Year	Total	First Prize
1860	nil	nil
1863	10	nil
1864	16	6
1876	27	10
1889	22	8
1891	28.50	10
1892	110	(Amateur winner)
1893	100	30
1910	125	50
1920	225	75
1927	275	100
1930	400	100
1931	500	100
1946	1,000	150
1949	1,700	300
1953	2,450	500
1954	3,500	750
1955	3,750	1,000
1958	4,850	1,000
1959	5,000	1,000
1960	7,000	1,250
1961	8,500	1,400
1963	8,500	1,500
1965	10,000	1,750
1966	15,000	2,100
1968	20,000	3,000
1969	30,000	4,250
1970	40,000	5,250
1971	45,000	5,500
1972	50,000	5,500
1975	75,000	7,500
1977	100,000	10,000
1978	125,000	12,500
1979	155,000	15,500
1980	200,000	25,000
1982	250,000	32,000
1983	300,000	40,000
1984	451,000	55,000
1985	530,000	65,000
1986	600,000	70,000
1987	650,000	75,000
1988	700,000	80,000
1989	750,000	80,000
1990	825,000	85,000
1991	900,000	90,000
1992	950,000	95,000
1993	1,000,000	100,000
1994	1,100,000	110,000
1995	1,250,000	125,000
1996	1,400,000	200,000
1997	1,600,000	250,000
1998	1,800,000	300,000
1999	2,000,000	350,000

ATTENDANCE

Year	Attendance
1962	37,098
1963	24,585
1964	35,954
1965	32,927
1966	40,182
1967	29,880
1968	51,819
1969	46,001
1970	81,593
1971	70,076
1972	84,746
1973	78,810
1974	92,796
1975	85,258
1976	92,021
1977	87,615
1978	125,271
1979	134,501
1980	131,610
1981	111,987
1982	133,299
1983	142,892
1984	193,126
1985	141,619
1986	134,261
1987	139,189
1988	191,334
1989	160,639
1990	208,680
1991	189,435
1992	146,427
1993	141,000
1994	128,000
1995	180,000
1996	171,000
1997	176,000
1998	195,100
1999	157,000

COMPLETE SCORES

128TH OPEN CHAMPIONSHIP

*Denotes amateurs

		1	2	3	4	5	6	7	8	9	10	11	12	13	14	15	16	17	18	
HOLE																				
PAR		4	4	4	4	4	5	4	3	4	4	4	4	3	5	4	3	4	4	**TOTAL**
Paul Lawrie	Round 1	4	4	4	4	4	5	5	3	4	4	4	3	4	5	5	3	4	4	73
Scotland	Round 2	4	5	4	5	4	5	4	3	4	3	4	5	4	4	4	3	5	4	74
£350,000	Round 3	5	5	3	5	4	6	5	3	4	4	4	3	5	4	4	3	4	5	76
	Round 4	4	4	3	4	5	4	4	2	4	4	4	3	4	4	4	3	3	4	67-290
	Play-off															5	4	3	3	15
Justin Leonard	Round 1	4	4	3	4	4	6	5	3	4	4	4	5	3	5	4	3	4	4	73
USA	Round 2	4	4	4	4	4	5	5	3	5	5	4	5	2	4	4	4	4	4	74
£185,000	Round 3	4	4	4	3	4	4	5	2	4	5	4	5	3	4	4	4	4	4	71
	Round 4	4	4	4	4	4	4	4	3	4	5	4	4	3	4	5	3	4	5	72-290
	Play-off															5	4	4	5	18
Jean Van de Velde	Round 1	5	4	4	4	4	5	4	3	3	4	5	5	3	3	5	4	6	4	75
France	Round 2	4	4	4	4	4	4	3	3	4	4	4	4	4	5	4	2	4	3	68
£185,000	Round 3	4	5	3	5	4	5	3	3	4	4	4	5	3	4	4	3	4	3	70
	Round 4	4	5	5	4	4	5	4	4	3	4	5	5	3	4	4	3	4	7	77-290
	Play-off															6	4	3	5	18
Angel Cabrera	Round 1	5	5	4	4	4	5	4	3	5	4	4	3	3	5	5	3	5	4	75
Argentina	Round 2	4	3	4	4	4	6	4	2	4	4	4	4	3	4	4	2	5	4	69
£100,000	Round 3	4	5	4	4	5	7	4	3	4	4	4	4	3	4	5	4	4	5	77
	Round 4	4	4	3	4	4	5	4	3	4	4	3	4	4	5	4	3	4	4	70-291
Craig Parry	Round 1	6	4	4	5	4	5	4	3	4	4	4	5	3	4	5	3	5	4	76
Australia	Round 2	4	5	4	3	4	5	5	3	4	3	4	6	3	4	5	4	4	5	75
£100,000	Round 3	4	4	3	3	4	4	4	3	4	4	3	5	4	3	4	2	5	4	67
	Round 4	4	4	3	4	4	5	4	2	4	3	4	7	4	5	4	3	6	3	73-291
Greg Norman	Round 1	6	4	4	4	5	5	3	3	5	4	5	5	3	4	4	3	5	4	76
Australia	Round 2	4	4	4	3	4	5	4	3	4	4	4	3	2	4	4	3	7	4	70
£70,000	Round 3	3	5	5	4	4	4	5	3	4	5	4	5	3	4	4	3	5	5	75
	Round 4	4	4	4	5	5	5	4	3	4	4	4	3	3	4	4	3	4	5	72-293
Davis Love III	Round 1	4	4	4	4	4	5	3	3	4	4	4	6	4	5	5	3	4	4	74
USA	Round 2	4	5	4	3	4	5	5	5	4	4	5	4	2	6	4	3	5	4	74
£50,000	Round 3	4	6	3	5	3	6	5	5	5	5	5	5	3	4	4	3	4	4	77
	Round 4	4	3	4	3	4	5	3	4	5	5	3	5	2	4	4	4	4	3	69-294
Tiger Woods	Round 1	4	4	4	5	5	5	4	3	4	4	4	4	3	4	4	4	5	4	74
USA	Round 2	3	4	4	3	5	5	2	4	4	5	5	3	4	4	4	4	4	5	72
£50,000	Round 3	4	4	4	4	4	5	5	3	4	4	4	4	3	5	4	3	6	4	74
	Round 4	4	4	4	4	4	5	4	3	4	4	4	6	3	4	5	3	4	5	74-294

HOLE		1	2	3	4	5	6	7	8	9	10	11	12	13	14	15	16	17	18	
PAR		4	4	4	4	4	5	4	3	4	4	4	4	3	5	4	3	4	4	TOTAL
David Frost	Round 1	4	5	5	6	5	5	5	3	5	4	3	6	3	5	4	4	4	4	80
South Africa	Round 2	4	4	3	4	4	5	4	4	4	4	4	4	3	4	4	3	4	3	69
£50,000	Round 3	4	4	3	4	4	6	5	2	4	5	4	5	3	4	3	3	4	4	71
	Round 4	5	6	3	5	6	4	3	3	4	4	4	5	2	4	4	4	4	4	74-294
Jim Furyk	Round 1	4	4	5	4	4	5	4	3	6	4	4	5	3	4	5	4	5	5	78
USA	Round 2	4	4	4	3	4	5	4	3	4	4	4	5	2	4	5	3	4	5	71
£34,800	Round 3	4	4	4	4	5	6	5	3	4	4	5	5	3	5	4	3	4	4	76
	Round 4	4	3	3	4	4	5	4	3	3	5	4	3	3	4	6	4	4	4	70-295
Scott Dunlap	Round 1	4	4	4	3	4	6	4	3	4	4	4	4	3	4	5	4	4	4	72
USA	Round 2	5	3	5	3	4	5	5	4	5	4	5	4	3	4	4	5	5	4	77
£34,800	Round 3	5	4	4	4	4	8	4	3	4	4	4	4	3	4	4	4	5	4	76
	Round 4	3	3	4	4	5	6	4	4	4	4	4	4	2	4	4	2	4	5	70-295
Retief Goosen	Round 1	4	4	4	4	5	6	4	4	6	4	4	5	2	4	5	3	4	4	76
South Africa	Round 2	4	3	5	6	4	6	4	3	4	3	5	5	3	5	4	3	5	3	75
£34,800	Round 3	4	4	5	5	4	5	4	3	4	5	4	4	3	4	4	3	4	4	73
	Round 4	4	4	5	4	4	5	3	3	4	5	4	4	3	4	4	3	4	4	71-295
Jesper Parnevik	Round 1	4	3	4	4	4	5	4	3	5	6	5	5	2	5	4	3	4	4	74
Sweden	Round 2	4	4	4	5	4	6	3	2	4	3	4	4	3	5	4	3	5	4	71
£34,800	Round 3	4	4	4	5	4	5	4	3	5	5	7	4	3	4	5	3	5	4	78
	Round 4	5	4	3	4	5	4	4	4	4	4	3	6	2	4	4	3	3	6	72-295
Hal Sutton	Round 1	4	4	4	5	3	5	6	2	4	4	4	4	3	4	5	4	4	4	73
USA	Round 2	4	5	4	5	3	6	4	4	5	5	4	4	4	5	5	3	4	4	78
£34,800	Round 3	4	4	4	4	4	6	4	2	5	4	4	4	2	5	4	3	4	5	72
	Round 4	3	4	4	4	4	5	5	4	3	3	3	4	4	5	4	3	4	6	72-295
Scott Verplank	Round 1	4	4	4	6	4	6	4	3	4	5	4	6	4	4	5	4	5	4	80
USA	Round 2	4	4	4	4	4	7	4	3	5	4	4	4	3	5	4	3	4	4	74
£26,000	Round 3	4	3	4	5	4	5	4	3	4	5	4	3	4	4	4	3	6	4	73
	Round 4	4	3	4	5	4	4	4	3	4	4	4	4	2	4	4	3	4	5	69-296
Tsuyoshi Yoneyama	Round 1	4	5	4	4	6	5	4	3	5	5	4	4	3	4	4	4	5	4	77
Japan	Round 2	4	4	4	7	4	5	5	3	4	4	4	5	2	3	4	4	4	4	74
£26,000	Round 3	4	4	4	3	4	5	4	4	5	4	4	5	3	4	4	4	4	4	73
	Round 4	4	3	4	4	5	4	4	4	5	5	4	4	3	4	5	3	4	3	72-296
Colin Montgomerie	Round 1	4	4	4	3	5	6	4	5	4	3	5	4	3	4	3	4	4	5	74
Scotland	Round 2	5	4	4	4	4	5	5	4	4	3	5	4	3	4	5	4	5	4	76
£26,000	Round 3	4	4	4	4	3	6	5	3	3	4	3	4	3	4	5	4	5	4	72
	Round 4	5	4	4	4	4	5	4	3	3	7	4	4	3	5	4	3	4	4	74-296
Lee Westwood	Round 1	4	4	4	5	4	5	5	4	4	3	4	4	3	4	4	4	6	5	76
England	Round 2	4	4	4	4	5	6	4	3	3	4	4	5	3	6	4	3	4	5	75
£20,500	Round 3	4	6	4	4	4	6	5	3	5	3	4	4	3	4	3	3	4	5	74
	Round 4	3	4	4	4	4	6	4	4	4	4	4	4	3	5	4	3	4	4	72-297
Costantino Rocca	Round 1	4	4	4	5	5	5	6	2	5	5	5	5	3	5	5	3	3	7	81
Italy	Round 2	4	4	3	5	4	4	4	3	5	4	4	3	2	4	3	4	4	5	69
£20,500	Round 3	4	5	4	5	4	5	4	3	4	4	4	5	3	4	5	3	4	4	74
	Round 4	4	4	3	4	4	6	4	3	5	5	5	4	2	4	4	3	5	4	73-297
Patrik Sjoland	Round 1	3	4	3	3	6	6	4	4	4	4	5	4	3	4	4	3	7	3	74
Sweden	Round 2	4	4	4	4	4	5	5	3	5	3	4	6	3	4	4	2	4	4	72
£20,500	Round 3	3	4	3	5	4	5	5	4	5	5	4	4	4	5	4	4	4	5	77
	Round 4	4	4	4	4	4	6	3	3	3	4	3	5	5	6	5	3	4	4	74-297

HOLE		1	2	3	4	5	6	7	8	9	10	11	12	13	14	15	16	17	18	
PAR		4	4	4	4	4	5	4	3	4	4	4	4	3	5	4	3	4	4	TOTAL
Bernhard Langer	Round 1	4	3	4	4	3	7	4	2	4	4	5	4	3	4	4	4	5	4	72
Germany	Round 2	4	4	4	3	5	5	5	4	4	5	4	4	3	4	5	4	5	5	77
£20,500	Round 3	5	4	4	4	4	5	4	2	5	5	4	4	3	4	5	3	4	4	73
	Round 4	4	4	3	4	5	5	4	3	5	4	3	5	3	4	5	3	5	6	75-297
Frank Nobilo	Round 1	4	4	6	5	4	6	4	3	4	4	4	5	3	4	5	3	4	4	76
New Zealand	Round 2	4	4	4	4	4	6	5	3	5	4	5	5	3	4	4	3	5	4	76
£20,500	Round 3	4	4	4	4	3	5	4	2	5	5	4	4	2	4	4	3	5	4	70
	Round 4	4	4	4	4	5	6	4	3	4	5	4	5	3	4	5	3	4	4	75-297
Andrew Coltart	Round 1	4	4	4	4	5	5	4	2	4	4	4	4	3	4	5	4	6	5	74
Scotland	Round 2	4	3	3	4	4	6	5	4	4	4	4	5	3	4	4	3	5	5	74
£20,500	Round 3	4	4	4	4	3	5	5	3	4	4	4	4	3	4	4	4	5	4	72
	Round 4	4	5	4	4	4	6	5	3	5	4	4	5	3	5	4	3	4	5	77-297
Ernie Els	Round 1	3	4	6	4	5	6	3	3	5	5	4	3	4	4	4	4	3	4	74
South Africa	Round 2	6	4	4	5	4	5	4	3	5	4	4	4	3	5	4	3	4	5	76
£15,300	Round 3	4	4	4	5	3	7	5	4	5	3	4	4	3	5	4	3	5	4	76
	Round 4	4	4	3	5	4	6	5	3	4	5	4	4	3	4	4	3	3	4	72-298
Peter O'Malley	Round 1	4	3	5	5	4	6	4	4	6	4	5	4	2	5	4	3	4	4	76
Australia	Round 2	5	4	4	4	5	6	5	3	4	4	3	5	3	4	4	3	6	3	75
£15,300	Round 3	4	4	5	4	5	5	4	3	4	4	4	4	4	4	4	4	4	4	74
	Round 4	3	4	4	4	4	4	4	2	4	6	5	6	3	5	4	3	4	4	73-298
Brian Watts	Round 1	5	4	4	4	4	6	5	3	5	4	3	4	3	4	4	4	4	4	74
USA	Round 2	4	6	4	4	4	5	4	4	4	3	4	5	3	4	4	4	4	3	73
£15,300	Round 3	5	4	3	6	6	5	4	3	3	7	3	6	3	5	3	3	5	3	77
	Round 4	4	4	4	5	5	5	4	4	4	5	4	4	3	5	4	3	3	4	74-298
Ian Woosnam	Round 1	4	5	5	4	6	4	5	3	4	4	5	4	3	4	4	3	4	5	76
Wales	Round 2	4	4	4	3	4	6	3	4	4	5	4	5	2	4	5	3	5	5	74
£15,300	Round 3	4	4	4	5	4	7	5	3	4	4	4	4	2	5	5	3	3	4	74
	Round 4	4	4	4	4	4	4	4	4	4	4	4	5	3	4	6	3	4	5	74-298
Miguel Angel Martin	Round 1	4	4	4	4	4	5	4	3	4	4	4	4	3	5	4	4	5	5	74
Spain	Round 2	4	4	3	4	4	6	4	2	5	4	4	4	4	5	5	5	5	4	76
£15,300	Round 3	4	4	4	4	4	5	4	3	5	4	4	5	3	5	3	3	4	4	72
	Round 4	3	4	5	5	5	5	4	3	5	5	4	4	3	4	5	3	4	5	76-298
Padraig Harrington	Round 1	4	4	4	6	3	7	4	2	4	4	6	5	2	5	5	2	5	5	77
Ireland	Round 2	4	4	5	4	4	5	4	4	4	4	4	5	3	4	4	4	3	5	74
£13,500	Round 3	4	4	4	4	3	6	5	3	4	4	5	4	3	4	4	4	4	5	74
	Round 4	4	4	4	4	5	4	4	3	4	4	3	4	3	5	5	3	5	6	74-299
Pierre Fulke	Round 1	4	3	5	5	4	6	4	3	5	4	6	4	3	4	5	3	5	3	75
Sweden	Round 2	4	4	4	5	4	7	5	3	4	5	4	4	3	4	3	4	4	4	75
£11,557	Round 3	4	5	4	4	5	5	4	3	6	4	5	4	3	4	4	3	5	5	77
	Round 4	4	5	5	3	5	4	4	3	4	4	4	6	3	5	4	3	3	4	73-300
Darren Clarke	Round 1	4	4	4	4	5	6	4	5	5	4	4	5	3	3	4	4	4	4	76
N. Ireland	Round 2	5	5	4	3	4	8	5	3	4	3	4	5	3	4	5	3	4	3	75
£11,557	Round 3	4	3	4	4	5	6	4	3	5	4	5	5	2	5	5	3	5	4	76
	Round 4	4	4	4	4	4	5	4	4	4	4	3	4	3	5	5	3	4	5	73-300
Thomas Bjorn	Round 1	5	4	5	4	4	7	5	3	5	5	4	3	3	4	5	3	5	5	79
Denmark	Round 2	5	4	4	4	4	5	3	3	4	5	4	4	3	4	5	4	4	4	73
£11,557	Round 3	6	4	4	4	4	5	4	4	4	5	4	4	3	4	4	4	4	4	75
	Round 4	5	6	5	4	4	5	4	4	4	4	3	4	3	4	4	3	3	4	73-300

HOLE		1	2	3	4	5	6	7	8	9	10	11	12	13	14	15	16	17	18	
PAR		4	4	4	4	4	5	4	3	4	4	4	4	3	5	4	3	4	4	TOTAL
Jeff Maggert	Round 1	4	3	5	4	4	6	4	3	5	4	4	5	3	5	5	3	4	4	75
USA	Round 2	4	5	4	4	4	5	4	3	5	3	6	5	3	5	5	3	4	5	77
£11,557	Round 3	4	4	3	5	5	5	5	4	5	4	4	4	2	5	5	3	4	4	75
	Round 4	4	4	4	3	4	6	6	2	3	4	5	4	3	4	5	3	4	5	73-300
Payne Stewart	Round 1	4	4	4	5	5	5	5	4	4	4	5	6	2	4	5	4	5	4	79
USA	Round 2	4	4	4	4	4	5	4	3	5	5	4	4	3	4	4	3	4	5	73
£11,557	Round 3	3	4	5	5	4	5	4	2	5	4	4	5	3	4	4	3	5	5	74
	Round 4	3	5	4	5	3	6	4	3	4	4	4	5	3	4	4	4	5	4	74-300
Tim Herron	Round 1	5	4	5	4	5	6	5	3	5	5	5	5	4	5	4	3	4	4	81
USA	Round 2	4	3	3	4	3	5	4	3	5	4	5	4	2	5	5	3	4	4	70
£11,557	Round 3	5	4	3	5	4	5	6	2	3	5	4	4	3	4	5	3	5	4	74
	Round 4	4	4	3	4	4	6	3	4	5	4	4	5	4	4	5	4	4	4	75-300
Len Mattiace	Round 1	4	4	4	5	5	5	4	3	3	4	4	4	3	4	5	4	3	5	73
USA	Round 2	5	5	4	4	5	5	4	3	6	4	4	4	3	3	3	3	6	3	74
£11,557	Round 3	4	4	6	5	5	5	5	2	4	5	4	4	3	4	4	3	4	4	75
	Round 4	4	4	5	4	5	5	4	3	4	5	4	7	3	5	5	3	4	4	78-300
Peter Baker	Round 1	4	4	5	4	5	5	4	3	5	5	4	5	3	6	5	4	3	3	77
England	Round 2	4	4	4	5	4	6	5	3	4	4	4	4	3	4	4	2	4	6	74
£9,500	Round 3	5	5	4	4	4	6	6	3	4	5	4	4	3	5	6	3	4	3	78
	Round 4	4	4	3	4	4	5	3	3	4	4	4	4	3	6	4	3	5	5	72-301
Paul Affleck	Round 1	4	6	4	4	5	5	5	3	4	6	4	6	3	4	4	4	4	4	79
Wales	Round 2	4	4	4	4	6	6	5	3	3	4	4	5	3	4	4	4	4	4	75
£9,500	Round 3	4	4	4	4	4	4	6	3	4	5	4	4	3	4	5	4	4	4	74
	Round 4	5	3	4	4	4	5	5	3	4	5	4	4	2	4	5	4	4	4	73-301
Dudley Hart	Round 1	5	4	3	5	3	5	6	3	5	4	4	4	3	4	4	4	3	4	73
USA	Round 2	4	5	5	4	4	5	4	4	7	3	4	5	3	4	5	3	6	4	79
£9,500	Round 3	5	5	5	5	4	5	4	3	4	4	4	4	2	5	4	4	4	4	75
	Round 4	4	4	5	3	4	6	4	3	6	5	3	5	3	5	4	2	4	4	74-301
Mark McNulty	Round 1	3	3	4	4	4	6	4	3	5	4	5	5	3	5	3	4	4	4	73
Zimbabwe	Round 2	5	5	3	4	4	6	4	2	5	5	4	5	3	4	5	4	5	5	77
£9,500	Round 3	4	5	4	4	4	5	5	3	5	5	4	4	3	4	6	3	4	4	76
	Round 4	5	5	3	3	4	6	4	3	4	4	4	5	3	4	5	4	5	4	75-301
Michael Weir	Round 1	4	5	4	4	4	5	6	3	5	6	5	5	3	6	5	3	6	4	83
Canada	Round 2	3	4	5	4	6	5	3	3	5	5	4	4	2	4	4	3	3	4	71
£9,500	Round 3	4	4	4	3	4	5	6	3	3	5	4	4	2	5	4	4	4	4	72
	Round 4	4	5	4	4	5	6	4	3	5	4	4	5	2	5	5	2	4	4	75-301
Nick Price	Round 1	4	4	4	5	4	6	4	4	5	4	5	4	3	4	5	3	5	4	77
Zimbabwe	Round 2	4	4	3	5	4	6	5	4	4	4	6	4	2	4	4	3	5	3	74
£9,500	Round 3	4	4	3	7	4	5	5	3	4	4	4	4	3	4	4	3	4	4	73
	Round 4	4	5	4	5	5	5	5	3	4	3	5	5	4	4	4	3	4	5	77-301
Duffy Waldorf	Round 1	4	6	4	3	5	4	4	3	6	4	6	6	3	4	4	3	5	6	80
USA	Round 2	4	5	5	4	4	6	5	3	3	4	4	5	2	4	4	2	5	3	72
£8,700	Round 3	5	4	4	4	3	5	4	2	6	4	6	3	4	5	5	3	5	4	76
	Round 4	4	5	4	4	5	4	4	2	5	4	4	5	3	5	4	3	5	4	74-302
Mark James	Round 1	4	5	4	5	4	6	4	4	4	5	4	4	3	5	4	2	4	5	76
England	Round 2	3	5	3	5	4	6	4	4	4	4	5	5	3	5	4	2	4	4	74
£8,700	Round 3	5	4	4	4	4	4	4	2	3	4	5	6	4	5	4	4	5	3	74
	Round 4	4	4	4	4	3	7	4	3	5	6	4	5	3	5	4	3	5	5	78-302

HOLE		1	2	3	4	5	6	7	8	9	10	11	12	13	14	15	16	17	18	
PAR		4	4	4	4	4	5	4	3	4	4	4	4	3	5	4	3	4	4	TOTAL
David Howell	Round 1	4	4	4	5	5	5	5	4	5	4	5	4	3	4	4	3	4	4	76
England	Round 2	4	4	4	4	4	5	4	3	6	4	7	5	3	4	6	3	4	4	78
£8,113	Round 3	4	5	3	6	6	6	4	2	5	4	5	5	3	5	4	3	5	4	79
	Round 4	5	3	4	4	5	6	4	2	4	5	3	4	2	4	5	2	4	4	70-303
Jeff Sluman	Round 1	5	4	4	4	3	7	4	3	4	5	5	5	3	4	5	5	6	4	80
USA	Round 2	4	5	3	3	5	6	4	3	5	5	4	5	3	4	3	4	4	4	74
£8,113	Round 3	4	4	5	6	5	6	4	3	3	4	4	4	3	5	4	4	5	4	77
	Round 4	5	3	3	4	4	5	4	3	5	4	4	5	2	5	4	3	4	5	72-303
Steve Pate	Round 1	4	4	5	3	5	5	4	3	4	5	4	4	3	4	3	3	5	5	73
USA	Round 2	4	5	5	3	3	9	5	3	4	4	4	4	3	5	4	3	4	4	76
£8,113	Round 3	7	5	4	5	4	5	4	3	5	4	4	5	2	5	4	3	5	6	80
	Round 4	4	4	3	4	4	5	4	4	5	4	5	4	3	5	4	4	4	4	74-303
Naomichi Ozaki	Round 1	4	4	4	3	4	6	5	2	4	3	4	4	3	7	4	4	5	4	74
Japan	Round 2	5	4	4	5	4	5	5	3	4	4	5	5	3	5	5	4	4	4	78
£8,113	Round 3	4	4	4	4	4	5	4	4	4	4	4	4	3	4	6	3	6	4	75
	Round 4	4	4	4	5	4	5	5	3	5	4	4	4	3	5	4	4	3	6	76-303
Stephen Allan	Round 1	5	6	4	3	4	5	6	4	4	4	5	6	3	5	4	3	4	4	79
Australia	Round 2	4	4	4	4	4	5	3	3	4	4	4	5	3	4	5	3	6	4	73
£7,217	Round 3	5	5	4	5	5	6	4	3	5	4	4	6	3	5	5	3	7	4	83
	Round 4	4	4	3	3	4	4	4	4	5	4	4	4	2	5	4	2	4	5	69-304
Thomas Levet	Round 1	4	4	4	5	5	6	4	4	5	5	4	4	3	4	5	3	5	4	78
France	Round 2	4	5	4	5	4	6	4	3	5	3	4	5	3	4	4	4	5	4	76
£7,217	Round 3	5	5	4	4	4	5	3	4	4	4	4	4	3	5	4	3	5	6	76
	Round 4	3	4	4	5	4	4	4	3	4	4	5	5	3	5	5	4	4	4	74-304
Kyoung-ju Choi	Round 1	5	4	4	4	4	5	3	4	5	5	5	4	3	4	5	3	5	4	76
Korea	Round 2	4	4	4	4	5	6	5	3	4	3	3	4	3	4	4	3	4	5	72
£7,217	Round 3	4	4	3	6	6	7	5	3	6	4	4	5	3	5	4	3	4	5	81
	Round 4	5	4	4	5	4	5	4	3	4	4	3	5	3	4	5	3	4	6	75-304
Dean Robertson	Round 1	4	5	3	4	5	6	5	4	4	4	5	5	3	4	4	3	4	4	76
Scotland	Round 2	4	5	3	4	4	5	6	3	4	4	4	5	3	5	3	4	5	4	75
£7,217	Round 3	4	5	4	5	4	5	5	3	4	4	5	5	3	5	4	3	4	6	78
	Round 4	4	6	4	4	4	6	3	3	4	6	4	4	2	5	4	2	7	3	75-304
Neil Price	Round 1	4	5	4	5	4	6	6	3	5	4	3	5	3	4	4	3	6	5	79
England	Round 2	3	5	4	4	4	5	4	3	5	3	5	4	3	5	4	3	6	4	74
£7,217	Round 3	5	4	4	5	4	5	4	4	4	4	4	4	3	5	5	3	5	4	76
	Round 4	4	4	5	3	4	6	4	4	5	4	4	5	3	5	4	3	4	4	75-304
Katsuyoshi Tomori	Round 1	5	4	5	4	4	4	4	4	4	4	4	6	2	4	4	4	4	4	74
Japan	Round 2	4	4	4	5	4	5	4	4	5	4	4	4	3	4	4	4	5	4	75
£7,217	Round 3	4	5	4	4	4	6	5	3	4	5	5	5	3	4	5	4	4	5	79
	Round 4	4	3	4	4	5	5	4	3	5	5	5	4	3	4	5	3	5	5	76-304
Bob Estes	Round 1	5	4	4	4	4	5	4	3	5	4	5	4	4	5	4	3	4	4	75
USA	Round 2	4	4	5	4	4	6	5	2	5	4	4	4	3	5	5	3	5	4	76
£7,217	Round 3	4	4	2	4	4	5	5	4	7	5	4	4	3	4	4	4	4	6	77
	Round 4	6	4	4	4	6	5	4	3	4	4	6	4	3	5	4	3	4	3	76-304
Peter Lonard	Round 1	4	4	5	5	5	5	3	3	4	5	4	6	3	5	5	3	4	3	76
Australia	Round 2	3	4	4	4	4	6	5	3	4	5	6	5	3	5	4	4	5	4	78
£7,217	Round 3	5	4	4	4	4	5	5	3	4	5	5	4	3	4	4	3	5	3	74
	Round 4	4	4	4	4	4	5	5	4	5	4	4	4	3	6	4	3	5	4	76-304

HOLE		1	2	3	4	5	6	7	8	9	10	11	12	13	14	15	16	17	18	
PAR		4	4	4	4	4	5	4	3	4	4	4	4	3	5	4	3	4	4	TOTAL
Bradley Hughes	Round 1	4	4	4	5	4	6	4	4	5	3	4	5	3	4	5	3	5	4	76
Australia	Round 2	3	4	4	4	4	4	4	4	4	4	5	4	2	5	4	3	4	5	71
£7,217	Round 3	4	4	3	6	4	7	6	4	5	4	4	5	3	3	6	3	4	3	78
	Round 4	3	4	4	4	6	7	4	3	4	5	4	6	5	5	4	2	5	4	79-304
Santiago Luna	Round 1	6	5	4	5	4	6	5	5	4	2	4	6	2	4	4	4	4	4	78
Spain	Round 2	5	5	3	5	4	5	5	2	5	4	5	4	3	5	4	3	3	4	74
£6,563	Round 3	4	4	4	6	5	5	5	3	5	4	5	4	3	5	4	3	4	7	80
	Round 4	4	4	4	4	4	6	4	3	5	4	4	5	3	4	5	2	4	4	73-305
Dennis Paulson	Round 1	4	4	4	4	4	5	5	3	4	5	4	4	3	4	5	3	5	4	74
USA	Round 2	4	6	4	5	4	5	4	3	4	5	5	4	2	5	6	4	4	4	78
£6,563	Round 3	4	5	4	5	4	5	4	3	5	4	5	4	3	5	5	4	4	6	79
	Round 4	4	4	4	4	4	6	4	4	4	4	4	5	3	4	4	3	5	4	74-305
Phillip Price	Round 1	5	5	4	4	4	6	4	4	4	4	3	5	3	4	5	4	5	4	77
Wales	Round 2	3	5	3	4	4	6	4	3	6	4	4	5	3	5	4	4	5	5	76
£6,563	Round 3	4	4	3	5	4	5	4	4	5	4	5	4	3	4	5	3	7	4	77
	Round 4	5	4	5	4	4	5	4	4	5	4	3	4	2	4	5	3	6	4	75-305
Jeremy Robinson	Round 1	4	6	4	4	3	6	3	4	3	5	5	5	3	4	5	5	4	4	77
England	Round 2	5	6	4	4	4	6	4	3	4	5	4	4	3	4	4	3	4	5	76
£6,563	Round 3	4	5	4	5	4	6	4	3	5	4	3	5	3	4	4	3	5	6	77
	Round 4	3	3	4	4	3	5	5	3	6	6	4	4	3	6	4	4	4	4	75-305
David Duval	Round 1	4	3	5	5	4	6	4	4	4	4	4	5	3	6	5	4	5	4	79
USA	Round 2	4	3	4	4	4	7	4	3	4	4	4	4	3	3	5	4	6	5	75
£6,350	Round 3	5	5	4	4	4	5	6	3	4	5	5	4	2	4	4	3	5	4	76
	Round 4	4	5	3	4	5	7	3	3	5	5	4	5	2	4	4	3	5	5	76-306
Johan Rystrom	Round 1	5	5	4	4	5	5	5	3	5	3	5	4	3	4	5	4	5	4	78
Sweden	Round 2	5	5	4	4	4	5	4	4	4	4	4	4	2	5	4	4	4	5	75
£6,350	Round 3	6	3	4	5	4	6	4	4	4	4	4	4	3	4	5	3	5	4	76
	Round 4	3	4	4	4	4	5	4	3	4	7	4	4	3	6	6	4	3	5	77-306
Mark Brooks	Round 1	4	5	5	4	5	7	5	4	5	4	5	4	3	4	5	4	5	4	82
USA	Round 2	3	3	4	3	4	4	4	3	4	5	4	4	3	5	5	3	5	4	70
£6,350	Round 3	5	6	4	4	3	6	4	3	3	5	4	5	3	5	5	3	4	4	76
	Round 4	4	4	4	5	4	5	4	3	4	4	5	6	3	5	5	3	5	5	78-306
Jarmo Sandelin	Round 1	3	4	4	4	4	5	4	4	4	3	4	6	3	4	4	4	7	4	75
Sweden	Round 2	4	6	4	4	4	6	4	4	4	5	4	4	4	5	5	4	3	4	78
£6,250	Round 3	4	4	4	4	5	5	4	4	6	5	4	3	3	4	5	3	5	4	77
	Round 4	4	3	4	4	4	6	4	3	6	4	4	4	3	5	6	4	5	4	77-307
Sven Struver	Round 1	4	5	5	5	4	6	4	4	5	4	4	4	2	4	4	4	5	4	77
Germany	Round 2	5	4	3	4	4	6	4	2	4	5	4	3	2	5	4	4	5	5	73
£6,200	Round 3	5	4	4	4	4	5	5	3	5	6	5	6	3	4	5	3	4	4	79
	Round 4	5	5	4	4	4	5	5	3	4	4	7	5	3	4	4	4	4	5	79-308
Lee Thompson	Round 1	5	4	4	4	5	5	4	3	5	3	4	4	3	5	4	3	5	5	75
England	Round 2	5	4	3	5	3	5	4	4	5	6	4	5	3	5	4	3	5	5	78
£6,150	Round 3	5	5	4	4	4	5	4	4	4	5	4	4	3	4	3	4	6	4	76
	Round 4	3	4	4	5	4	5	5	3	5	4	4	5	3	8	6	4	3	5	80-309
Brian Davis	Round 1	5	4	4	4	4	5	6	3	6	6	4	4	3	4	5	3	5	5	80
England	Round 2	4	5	4	4	3	5	6	3	4	3	4	4	2	4	5	3	4	4	71
£6,075	Round 3	4	4	4	4	5	5	5	3	5	4	5	4	4	5	6	4	6	5	82
	Round 4	4	5	4	5	4	4	5	4	5	4	4	4	3	5	5	4	4	4	77-310

HOLE		1	2	3	4	5	6	7	8	9	10	11	12	13	14	15	16	17	18	
PAR		4	4	4	4	4	5	4	3	4	4	4	4	3	5	4	3	4	4	TOTAL
John Huston	Round 1	6	4	4	5	3	6	3	4	4	6	4	5	3	6	6	3	5	3	80
USA	Round 2	4	4	3	3	3	5	5	3	5	3	4	5	2	4	4	3	5	6	71
£6,075	Round 3	4	3	4	5	3	7	5	3	6	4	6	4	3	4	4	4	4	4	77
	Round 4	4	7	4	5	5	5	5	3	4	4	4	7	4	4	5	3	5	4	82-310
Lee Janzen	Round 1	4	4	4	6	5	6	4	2	5	4	4	5	3	5	5	4	5	5	80
USA	Round 2	5	4	4	3	4	5	4	4	3	4	5	5	4	4	3	3	6	4	74
£6,000	Round 3	4	4	4	4	5	4	5	3	6	4	4	4	2	4	8	4	6	4	79
	Round 4	4	5	4	4	5	4	4	4	5	5	4	6	3	4	5	3	4	5	78-311
Shingo Katayama	Round 1	4	4	4	5	5	6	4	4	4	4	4	4	3	5	5	3	4	4	76
Japan	Round 2	3	5	4	4	5	6	5	3	4	3	4	4	3	5	4	4	5	4	75
£6,000	Round 3	4	5	4	4	4	5	6	2	5	4	4	5	3	5	5	3	5	5	78
	Round 4	3	5	4	4	4	7	4	5	6	5	5	4	3	6	5	4	4	5	83-312
Martyn Thompson	Round 1	4	4	4	5	5	5	4	3	4	4	4	5	2	4	5	3	6	5	76
England	Round 2	5	5	3	4	4	6	5	3	4	5	4	5	3	4	5	4	4	5	78
£6,000	Round 3	5	4	4	4	4	5	5	3	4	5	4	5	3	4	4	4	6	5	78
	Round 4	4	4	4	5	5	6	6	4	5	5	4	4	3	5	5	4	4	4	81-313
Derrick Cooper	Round 1	3	4	4	4	4	5	5	3	5	3	5	3	3	4	5	3	7	5	75
England	Round 2	5	4	3	5	5	6	5	4	6	3	4	5	2	5	4	3	4	4	77
£6,000	Round 3	3	4	4	6	5	5	4	2	5	4	4	5	3	4	4	5	4	5	76
	Round 4	4	4	7	4	4	6	5	4	5	6	4	5	3	5	4	3	6	6	85-313

NON QUALIFIERS AFTER 36 HOLES

(Leading 10 professionals and ties receive £1,100 each, next 20 professionals and ties receive £900 each, next 20 professionals and ties receive £800 each, remainder of professionals receive £700 each.)

HOLE		1	2	3	4	5	6	7	8	9	10	11	12	13	14	15	16	17	18	
PAR		4	4	4	4	4	5	4	3	4	4	4	4	3	5	4	3	4	4	TOTAL
Scott Watson	Round 1	4	4	4	4	4	5	3	3	6	5	4	5	3	6	4	4	3	3	74
England	Round 2	5	4	4	6	4	8	4	3	4	5	4	4	3	4	4	4	5	6	81-155
Phil Mickelson	Round 1	4	5	4	4	5	5	4	3	4	5	7	4	3	5	5	4	4	4	79
USA	Round 2	4	4	4	5	5	6	4	3	5	4	4	4	4	4	4	3	5	4	76-155
Pedro Linhart	Round 1	4	4	4	4	5	6	5	4	5	5	5	4	3	5	6	3	4	4	80
Spain	Round 2	5	5	5	4	4	5	3	2	4	4	4	4	3	5	5	3	5	5	75-155
Craig Hainline	Round 1	4	4	4	5	4	5	5	3	5	5	4	4	2	4	5	4	4	4	75
USA	Round 2	5	4	4	5	4	5	6	3	5	4	4	6	4	4	4	3	5	5	80-155
Ross McFarlane	Round 1	5	4	5	3	4	5	4	3	5	5	5	5	3	5	4	3	4	5	77
England	Round 2	4	5	5	4	4	4	5	3	4	6	5	4	3	4	3	4	5	6	78-155
Tom Watson	Round 1	5	5	4	4	5	6	4	3	5	6	4	5	3	5	5	4	5	4	82
USA	Round 2	5	6	4	4	4	5	5	3	5	3	4	5	3	4	4	2	4	3	73-155
Miguel Angel Jimenez	Round 1	5	4	4	4	4	5	4	3	5	6	6	5	3	6	4	3	5	5	81
Spain	Round 2	4	5	4	4	5	4	5	2	5	4	4	4	3	5	4	3	5	4	74-155
Rocco Mediate	Round 1	3	4	4	4	5	5	6	4	4	4	4	4	3	6	5	4	5	4	79
USA	Round 2	4	5	4	4	5	5	4	2	4	4	4	6	2	5	5	3	4	6	76-155
Jean Hugo	Round 1	4	4	4	4	4	6	4	4	5	4	4	6	4	5	4	3	5	4	78
South Africa	Round 2	5	4	4	4	4	6	5	3	4	5	4	5	3	5	3	3	6	4	77-155
Per Nyman	Round 1	4	5	4	4	4	6	6	3	6	5	5	4	3	5	4	4	4	5	81
Sweden	Round 2	4	5	4	5	5	5	4	4	4	5	4	3	4	4	3	4	4	4	75-156
Andrew Magee	Round 1	5	5	4	4	4	6	5	4	4	5	4	4	3	4	4	4	4	4	77
USA	Round 2	5	5	4	5	5	6	5	4	4	3	4	4	4	4	4	4	4	5	79-156
Hidemichi Tanaka	Round 1	6	5	5	5	5	7	5	3	5	4	3	5	4	4	4	3	4	5	82
Japan	Round 2	4	4	4	4	6	5	4	3	5	4	6	4	3	4	4	2	4	4	74-156
Bob Tway	Round 1	3	4	5	4	4	5	4	4	4	4	5	6	2	4	4	4	4	5	75
USA	Round 2	5	3	3	5	4	5	5	5	5	6	4	6	4	4	4	3	5	5	81-156
Greg Turner	Round 1	3	5	4	4	4	6	5	3	5	3	6	4	3	5	5	3	5	5	78
New Zealand	Round 2	3	5	4	4	4	7	5	4	5	5	4	3	3	5	3	5	5	5	78-156
Corey Pavin	Round 1	5	3	4	4	4	6	6	4	4	4	5	4	4	6	5	3	4	5	80
USA	Round 2	4	4	4	4	5	6	5	2	4	5	4	4	4	4	3	5	5	5	76-156
Michael Campbell	Round 1	5	4	4	4	5	6	4	3	6	4	4	4	5	5	4	4	4	4	79
New Zealand	Round 2	4	4	3	4	4	6	6	3	5	5	6	4	3	4	4	4	4	4	77-156
*Luke Donald	Round 1	4	4	4	4	5	5	6	4	5	4	5	5	3	4	4	4	6	4	80
England	Round 2	4	5	4	4	5	5	4	4	4	4	4	4	2	4	5	3	6	5	76-156
Andrew Raitt	Round 1	5	4	4	5	4	6	6	4	5	4	3	4	3	4	5	4	4	4	78
England	Round 2	4	3	5	4	4	5	5	4	4	5	4	5	4	5	4	4	4	5	78-156
Paul Eales	Round 1	5	4	4	4	4	5	5	4	5	5	5	3	4	3	5	5	3	5	78
England	Round 2	5	4	5	4	3	6	5	3	5	4	3	5	3	5	4	4	5	5	78-156
Carlos Franco	Round 1	4	4	4	4	5	5	4	3	5	5	4	4	4	6	5	4	5	5	80
Paraguay	Round 2	4	4	5	5	5	6	4	3	5	4	4	4	3	5	4	3	4	4	76-156
Tom Lehman	Round 1	4	4	4	5	4	5	4	5	5	4	4	4	3	4	3	4	4	6	76
USA	Round 2	5	4	4	5	5	6	6	3	5	4	4	4	3	6	4	4	4	4	80-156

HOLE		1	2	3	4	5	6	7	8	9	10	11	12	13	14	15	16	17	18	
PAR		4	4	4	4	4	5	4	3	4	4	4	4	3	5	4	3	4	4	TOTAL
Brandt Jobe	Round 1	4	4	4	5	4	5	4	3	5	5	5	4	3	6	5	3	3	5	77
USA	Round 2	4	4	4	4	3	8	4	3	5	4	5	4	2	6	5	3	6	5	79-156
Stephen Leaney	Round 1	4	4	4	4	5	5	5	3	5	5	4	6	3	4	4	4	5	5	79
Australia	Round 2	6	4	4	4	4	7	5	3	5	4	4	4	3	5	4	3	4	4	77-156
Justin Rose	Round 1	5	5	4	4	5	7	4	4	4	5	4	4	3	4	4	3	4	6	79
England	Round 2	4	5	5	4	4	6	4	3	5	5	5	5	3	4	4	3	4	4	77-156
Michael Long	Round 1	5	5	4	4	4	6	4	3	6	6	3	5	3	5	3	4	4	4	78
New Zealand	Round 2	4	4	4	4	5	5	3	3	4	5	4	7	3	6	5	4	4	4	78-156
Gilberto Morales	Round 1	4	5	5	5	5	5	4	4	5	4	4	3	3	5	4	5	5	5	80
Venezuela	Round 2	4	5	4	5	4	5	5	3	5	4	4	6	3	4	4	4	4	3	76-156
Nick Faldo	Round 1	4	4	6	5	5	5	6	4	4	4	5	4	3	4	5	3	3	4	78
England	Round 2	5	6	3	4	4	6	4	3	6	5	5	4	3	4	4	4	5	4	79-157
Des Smyth	Round 1	4	4	4	4	4	5	4	3	5	5	5	4	3	5	5	3	4	4	75
Ireland	Round 2	5	4	6	4	5	5	5	3	6	4	5	4	3	5	5	4	4	5	82-157
Jose Maria Olazabal	Round 1	4	4	4	5	3	6	4	3	5	4	5	4	3	7	4	3	5	5	78
Spain	Round 2	4	5	3	5	3	6	5	3	5	5	5	5	3	5	5	3	5	4	79-157
Christopher Hanell	Round 1	5	4	4	6	5	5	4	4	6	5	4	4	3	6	4	3	4	5	81
Sweden	Round 2	5	4	4	4	4	5	5	3	5	4	4	4	3	4	6	3	5	4	76-157
Warren Bennett	Round 1	4	4	4	4	5	6	4	3	5	4	5	4	3	5	4	4	5	4	77
England	Round 2	4	5	4	4	4	5	5	3	4	4	5	5	3	6	5	5	4	5	80-157
Gabriel Hjertstedt	Round 1	5	4	4	4	5	5	6	3	6	4	6	5	2	4	5	3	4	4	79
Sweden	Round 2	4	4	4	4	4	4	6	5	6	4	5	4	2	5	5	3	5	4	78-157
Rodney Pampling	Round 1	4	4	4	4	4	5	4	3	4	4	4	5	2	3	5	3	5	4	71
Australia	Round 2	5	5	4	5	4	6	5	3	7	5	4	5	4	5	5	3	6	5	86-157
Steve Stricker	Round 1	5	4	4	5	5	5	4	2	5	6	4	4	4	5	5	3	5	5	80
USA	Round 2	4	6	4	3	3	5	4	4	5	4	4	5	2	5	5	4	5	5	77-157
Steve Elkington	Round 1	5	5	4	4	5	5	5	4	4	5	4	4	4	4	4	3	4	6	79
Australia	Round 2	4	4	5	4	4	6	4	4	4	4	5	4	3	6	4	4	5	4	78-157
Mark O'Meara	Round 1	4	6	6	4	4	6	5	4	4	6	5	4	3	4	5	3	7	3	83
USA	Round 2	5	4	4	5	4	6	4	3	4	4	4	4	4	5	3	3	4	4	74-157
Mathias Gronberg	Round 1	4	4	4	4	4	7	4	3	5	4	4	5	2	5	5	4	6	5	79
Sweden	Round 2	5	4	3	4	4	6	4	4	4	5	5	4	3	5	5	3	6	5	79-158
David Park	Round 1	4	4	5	4	5	6	4	2	6	4	4	4	3	4	6	3	4	5	77
Wales	Round 2	4	4	4	5	5	7	4	4	4	5	4	5	3	5	6	3	4	5	81-158
Shigeki Maruyama	Round 1	5	4	5	4	4	5	5	4	4	5	5	4	3	5	4	4	4	4	78
Japan	Round 2	4	4	4	5	4	5	4	4	5	6	4	3	4	5	4	4	4	7	80-158
Glen Day	Round 1	4	4	4	4	4	6	4	5	5	6	4	4	3	6	3	3	4	6	79
USA	Round 2	4	4	4	4	6	6	5	4	4	4	4	5	2	4	5	4	5	5	79-158
Robert Karlsson	Round 1	6	4	5	5	4	5	4	4	4	5	5	4	3	4	4	2	5	3	76
Sweden	Round 2	4	4	4	6	4	7	3	5	6	4	5	5	3	4	5	3	6	4	82-158
Richard Green	Round 1	5	6	5	5	4	6	4	3	5	4	4	4	4	5	6	3	5	3	81
Australia	Round 2	5	4	4	5	4	4	5	3	4	6	5	6	3	3	5	3	4	4	77-158
Scott Gump	Round 1	4	5	5	5	4	6	6	7	7	4	4	4	4	4	4	4	4	4	85
USA	Round 2	4	4	3	5	6	6	4	3	4	3	4	4	3	4	4	3	5	5	74-159
Jong-duck Kim	Round 1	4	4	5	5	5	6	7	4	4	5	5	5	3	4	4	3	4	6	83
Korea	Round 2	4	4	4	4	3	5	4	4	5	3	4	5	3	5	6	3	5	5	76-159

HOLE		1	2	3	4	5	6	7	8	9	10	11	12	13	14	15	16	17	18	
PAR		4	4	4	4	4	5	4	3	4	4	4	4	3	5	4	3	4	4	TOTAL
Jarrod Moseley	Round 1	4	5	4	6	4	5	6	4	4	5	5	5	3	5	5	4	4	7	85
Australia	Round 2	5	4	4	4	4	6	5	3	4	4	4	4	3	4	4	4	5	3	74-159
Greg Owen	Round 1	4	5	4	4	4	6	5	4	6	4	4	5	3	4	4	4	4	4	78
England	Round 2	5	6	4	4	4	5	7	3	5	6	5	5	2	5	4	4	4	3	81-159
Mark Calcavecchia	Round 1	5	4	4	4	3	7	5	3	5	5	4	5	3	6	4	3	4	4	78
USA	Round 2	5	3	5	5	4	7	5	3	5	4	4	5	4	4	5	4	4	5	81-159
Stuart Appleby	Round 1	4	5	4	4	3	5	5	3	4	5	4	4	3	4	4	4	5	8	78
Australia	Round 2	5	4	4	5	4	6	6	3	4	4	5	4	4	5	4	4	7	3	81-159
David Carter	Round 1	5	4	5	5	4	5	4	3	5	5	4	4	3	4	4	4	5	6	79
England	Round 2	4	4	4	4	4	5	5	4	4	4	5	6	4	4	4	5	6	4	80-159
Billy Andrade	Round 1	4	4	4	5	3	7	5	3	4	4	4	4	3	5	5	3	4	4	75
USA	Round 2	4	5	4	4	5	7	5	7	3	4	4	5	3	5	5	3	5	6	84-159
Geoff Ogilvy	Round 1	4	4	4	4	5	7	6	3	4	4	4	4	5	5	5	4	4	5	81
Australia	Round 2	4	3	4	4	4	6	5	2	4	6	3	4	3	4	5	4	7	6	78-159
Fabrice Tarnaud	Round 1	3	4	4	5	6	7	4	3	4	5	4	5	3	5	5	3	5	5	80
France	Round 2	6	5	4	4	4	5	5	3	4	4	4	4	3	6	5	5	4	4	79-159
Craig Spence	Round 1	4	4	5	4	4	5	4	4	5	5	4	5	4	5	4	5	5	5	81
Australia	Round 2	5	5	4	4	4	5	5	2	4	5	4	6	3	4	5	3	5	6	79-160
Raymond Russell	Round 1	4	5	6	5	4	7	4	3	5	4	4	5	3	4	4	4	6	5	82
Scotland	Round 2	4	4	4	4	5	5	4	3	5	5	5	5	3	5	4	4	4	5	78-160
*Paddy Gribben	Round 1	4	4	4	5	5	4	4	4	4	5	4	4	4	5	3	3	4	5	75
Ireland	Round 2	5	5	4	6	5	5	6	3	5	4	4	5	3	6	4	4	5	6	85-160
Paul McGinley	Round 1	5	5	4	4	6	6	6	4	6	4	5	5	3	5	4	3	4	4	83
Ireland	Round 2	4	5	4	4	5	5	5	5	3	4	5	4	2	4	4	4	6	4	77-160
Per-Ulrik Johansson	Round 1	5	4	4	4	4	5	4	4	6	5	6	5	3	4	5	3	4	4	79
Sweden	Round 2	4	4	4	4	4	8	6	4	4	4	5	4	4	4	5	4	4	4	81-160
Jon Bevan	Round 1	4	5	4	5	6	8	5	2	5	5	3	4	3	5	5	3	5	4	81
England	Round 2	3	5	3	5	4	6	5	4	5	4	5	5	3	5	5	3	5	5	80-161
Billy Mayfair	Round 1	4	4	4	4	4	7	5	4	4	5	4	5	2	5	5	3	6	6	81
USA	Round 2	4	4	4	4	4	6	6	3	5	4	5	5	4	4	4	4	5	5	80-161
Vijay Singh	Round 1	4	4	5	4	5	5	4	3	4	5	5	5	3	5	4	3	4	5	77
Fiji	Round 2	4	6	4	5	4	5	5	3	5	5	5	5	4	6	3	5	6		84-161
*Graeme Storm	Round 1	5	5	5	4	5	5	4	3	4	5	5	6	4	4	5	3	5	5	82
England	Round 2	3	4	4	5	5	6	4	5	5	4	4	5	3	4	4	4	5	5	79-161
Rich Beem	Round 1	5	5	4	5	4	5	3	4	7	5	4	4	3	5	6	3	4	4	80
USA	Round 2	5	4	3	6	4	6	5	4	6	4	5	5	4	5	4	2	4	5	81-161
Stephen Gallacher	Round 1	5	5	4	5	4	5	5	3	6	5	4	6	4	4	5	4	4	4	82
Scotland	Round 2	4	6	5	4	5	6	5	3	4	5	5	4	4	5	4	3	3	4	79-161
Marc Farry	Round 1	4	4	5	4	5	5	4	5	7	4	6	4	4	4	4	4	4	5	82
France	Round 2	5	5	5	4	5	7	4	3	5	5	4	5	3	4	3	3	4	5	79-161
Stewart Cink	Round 1	4	4	5	5	6	5	6	3	5	4	5	4	3	5	5	3	5	5	82
USA	Round 2	5	5	4	5	4	4	5	4	4	4	4	4	4	5	7	3	5	4	80-162
Ted Tryba	Round 1	5	3	4	5	4	5	4	4	5	4	5	5	3	5	4	5	5	5	80
USA	Round 2	6	3	4	5	5	6	4	3	5	6	5	4	4	5	4	4	5	82-162
*Zane Scotland	Round 1	5	4	5	4	7	6	5	3	4	5	5	5	2	4	4	3	5	7	82
England	Round 2	4	5	3	4	4	7	5	3	5	5	4	5	3	5	5	4	4	6	81-163

HOLE		1	2	3	4	5	6	7	8	9	10	11	12	13	14	15	16	17	18	
PAR		4	4	4	4	4	5	4	3	4	4	4	4	3	5	4	3	4	4	TOTAL
Gary Player	Round 1	4	5	5	4	8	5	5	4	4	4	5	3	3	4	4	3	6	5	81
South Africa	Round 2	4	5	4	5	4	5	4	4	7	4	5	5	3	6	5	4	5	4	83-164
Bob Charles	Round 1	6	4	4	4	5	5	6	3	5	4	5	4	4	5	6	3	5	5	83
New Zealand	Round 2	6	4	4	5	4	6	5	3	4	4	4	6	3	5	6	3	5	4	81-164
Kazuhiko Hosokawa	Round 1	5	5	4	5	6	6	5	3	3	6	4	5	4	4	5	4	5	4	83
Japan	Round 2	5	4	5	4	6	6	4	3	5	5	4	4	3	5	6	4	5	4	82-165
Allan MacDonald	Round 1	7	3	4	5	5	5	2	4	6	5	5	5	3	5	4	3	5	4	80
England	Round 2	5	5	5	6	6	6	5	3	5	5	5	4	4	4	4	4	3	5	85-165
Mark Allen	Round 1	5	6	4	5	4	6	4	3	5	5	5	4	4	5	3	4	4	4	80
Australia	Round 2	5	6	4	5	5	6	5	3	5	4	6	5	3	4	6	3	5	6	86-166
Anders Hansen	Round 1	4	4	5	4	4	8	4	3	5	5	4	6	4	6	5	4	4	3	82
Denmark	Round 2	5	4	4	5	4	6	4	3	5	3	4	8	4	5	5	4	6	5	84-166
Sandy Lyle	Round 1	4	4	4	4	5	6	6	4	6	5	5	4	4	3	4	4	7	6	85
Scotland	Round 2	5	5	5	5	5	5	3	3	4	5	5	5	3	4	5	3	7	4	81-166
Seve Ballesteros	Round 1	4	4	4	6	4	5	5	5	4	5	5	4	4	3	5	4	4	5	80
Spain	Round 2	6	4	5	4	5	5	5	3	5	7	4	6	3	4	5	3	6	6	86-166
Andrew Sherborne	Round 1	4	4	5	5	4	7	5	4	4	8	5	4	3	4	5	4	7	5	87
England	Round 2	4	6	4	4	5	6	4	4	5	5	5	4	3	5	4	4	4	4	80-167
Eduardo Herrera	Round 1	4	6	5	4	5	5	5	4	5	5	5	5	3	4	4	3	4	5	81
Argentina	Round 2	4	5	4	5	4	8	5	3	5	4	5	5	4	5	5	5	5	5	86-167
Tony Jacklin	Round 1	6	4	4	5	5	6	6	2	4	4	6	5	3	6	4	3	7	5	85
England	Round 2	4	5	4	5	5	6	4	3	5	4	5	6	3	5	5	4	5	4	82-167
Prayad Marksaeng	Round 1	5	5	4	7	5	7	5	4	7	6	5	4	3	7	4	3	4	6	91
Thailand	Round 2	5	4	4	4	5	5	5	4	4	5	4	5	4	4	4	4	4	5	79-170
Simon McCarthy	Round 1	4	5	5	5	4	6	5	4	5	6	4	5	3	6	4	3	4	4	82
England	Round 2	5	7	4	6	5	5	5	3	5	5	5	5	4	7	5	4	5	4	89-171
Sergio Garcia	Round 1	7	4	4	5	5	5	4	4	6	6	5	6	3	4	5	5	5	6	89
Spain	Round 2	5	5	4	5	4	5	6	3	6	4	6	5	4	5	5	3	4	4	83-172
Fred Funk	Round 1	4	4	3	4	4	6	6	3	5	5	5	6	4	6	4	3	5	6	83-WD
USA																				
Tom Gillis	Round 1	5	5	4	4	6	6	4	3	7	5	6	6	4	5	6	4	4	6	90-WD
USA																				

CARD OF THE CHAMPIONSHIP COURSE

Hole	Yards	Par	Hole	Yards	Par
1	407	4	10	466	4
2	462	4	11	383	4
3	342	4	12	479	4
4	412	4	13	169	3
5	411	4	14	515	5
6	578	5	15	472	4
7	412	4	16	250	3
8	183	3	17	459	4
9	474	4	18	487	4
Out	3681	36	In	3680	35
			Out	3681	36
			Total	7361	71

Barry Burn

CARNOUSTIE
GOLF LINKS